# KIDS MINISTRY 101:
## PRACTICAL ANSWERS TO QUESTIONS ABOUT KIDS MINISTRY

Published by LifeWay Press®
© 2009 LifeWay Press®

No part of this work may be reproduced or transmitted in any form or by any means, electronic or mechanical, including photocopying and recording, or by any information storage or retrieval system, except as may be expressly permitted in writing by the publisher. Request for permission should be addressed in writing to LifeWay Press®, One LifeWay Plaza, Nashville, TN 37234.

ISBN 1415867380
Item 005191563

The book is a resource for both the Preschool and Children's Leadership and Skill Development category of the Christian Growth Study Plan. Courses LS-0013, LS-0015, LS-0021, LS-0023, LS-0056, LS-0106

Dewey Decimal Classification Number 259.22
Subject Headings: CHURCH WORK WITH CHILDREN\ CHRISTIAN EDUCATION\ RELIGIOUS EDUCATION CHILDREN

Printed in the United States of America

Childhood Ministry Publishing
LifeWay Christian Resources
One LifeWay Plaza
Nashville, Tennessee 37234-0172

# Kids Ministry 101
# Table of Contents

# Why Kids Ministry 101?

So you are doing kids ministry in your church and sometimes wonder if you're doing the right things—the things that will really impact children and their families. That's what this book is all about. We want to help you get back to the basics of kids ministry and provide you with practical answers to the everyday questions many people ask as they develop this important, foundational ministry in their church.

This compilation represents some of the best thinkers in kids ministry today. These writers are not only experts but also are people who love children and have lots of personal experience in doing effective kids ministry in the local church. Like you, they teach kids, connect with families, and serve with other kids ministry workers. It is our prayer that their answers will be used by God to help equip you to transform the lives of children in your church, community, and possibly around the world.

LifeWay Kids Ministry Team

## LifeWay Kids Promise

At LifeWay, we work hard to know kids. We take time to understand how they play and how they learn. And we know you need resources you can trust to connect kids to God's Word—leading them toward knowing Christ and growing in relationship with Him. That's why LifeWay Kids promises to offer foundational resources that are biblically sound, age-appropriate, fun, and easy to use. These foundational resources help kids hear God's Word, know God's Word, and do God's Word by learning to apply it to their lives.

# Strategy?

**There's more to ministry than kids ?**

**A**fter Sunday School, Caryn took the helper chart I gave her to "big church" and covered it with stickers. Later, Caryn's mother reported that Caryn spent the week helping at home. When we catch a glimpse of a child's day and observe her doing God's Word, I wonder if we experience but a fraction of the pleasure God feels when we obey Him.

*Landry R. Holmes*

I know what I'm doing. I have it all planned out—plans to take care of you, not abandon you, plans to give you the future you hope for.

**Jeremiah 29:11**
**(The Message)**

# Chapter 1
# What Is the Church's Role in Kids Ministry?

*Some people were bringing little children to Him so He might touch them, but His disciples rebuked them. When Jesus saw it, He was indignant and said to them, "Let the little children come to Me. Don't stop them, for the kingdom of God belongs to such as these. I assure you: Whoever does not welcome the kingdom of God like a little child will never enter it." After taking them in His arms, He laid His hands on them and blessed them. Mark 10:13-16*

What is the church's role in ministry to kids? Why should churches have a kids ministry? Why do we invest time and money in our kids? Is ministry to boys and girls based on the child-care needs of their parents? Or is the greater question, "Have I been called to something far greater than baby-sitting?" These questions always cause me to reconsider God's calling on my life.

## What do you see when you look at the kids in your ministry?
I often ask God to help me see through His eyes. Do you ever look at the kids God has placed in your life and see doctors, teachers, homemakers, business executives, and firefighters? Do you see 2-year-olds playing with blocks and balls, or do you see pastors, deacons, Sunday School teachers, and worship leaders? I am convinced the future of the church is sitting in our preschool and children's classrooms today. Therefore, ministry to kids is actually preparation for the present and the future of the church and is certainly important.

There is no place in Scripture that specifically instructs the church as it relates to children. There is, however, a biblical mandate to parents to teach their children in the way they should go, to teach the precepts of God, to guide them to use the Bible, and to do it all with a healthy fear.

## If there is no scriptural instruction about kids ministry, does that mean the church is off the hook with no responsibility?
Definitely not! Children are a blessing from God, but with every blessing comes responsibility. It is our responsibility as part of the family of God to partner with parents in the great adventure of training up their kids.

It is our responsibility to work together as a community of believers to provide opportunities for children to grow in their relationships with God and with the church. Kids' attitudes regarding the church, their decisions to be active participants and contributors in church, and yes, even their view of and attitudes about God are formed in the preschool and children's classrooms. The ministry you provide to both kids and their parents plays a crucial role in creating positive experiences and memories that lay foundations for each child's future as a Christian and a church member. We also have the privilege of partnering with parents in their children's spiritual development. We can help nurture kids as they begin to understand God's plan of salvation, His personal call for them to accept His provision through the work of Jesus Christ, and the fact that God indeed has a special plan for each of them. We can teach the kids about their God-given gifts and talents and how those gifts fit into His church. Together, the body works to lay foundations of faith that are built upon in the context of a caring and nurturing environment.

By offering opportunities for parents to work together with the church, we multiply our efforts to ensure that each child is prepared adequately to take on the responsibility of leading now and in the future.

The church has the privilege of investing in its own future. Through discipleship opportunities such as small group Bible studies, corporate and congregational worship, Vacation Bible School, weekday programs, camps, and retreats, the church is preparing for its future. Ask yourself: "What kind of future do I want for my church?" Then ask: "Is God pleased with the future our church is preparing?"

### How does the church tackle this important task?
We are successful when we provide age-suitable, Bible-based opportunities that fit the God-given mission of the particular church God has placed us in. We can measure our success as we see boys and girls grow up to become strong, committed, and growing followers of Christ.

*Bill Emeott*

# Chapter 2

# What Is a Strategy for Kids Ministry?

*A man's heart plans his way, but the LORD determines his steps. Proverbs 16:9*

Looking around most churches, you will discover the "used-to-be's"—people who "used-to-be" preschool Sunday School teachers, who "used-to-be" elementary discipleship leaders. Why so many "used-to-be's" in our midst? One predominant cause is a failure to serve with a vision. Developing a strategy for your kids ministry is essential to ministering with a vision.

## What is a strategy?

When ministers and leaders begin to think about strategy, an old adage often comes to mind: "To fail to plan is to plan to fail." A *strategy* might best be defined as "a specific plan (doesn't need to be long or complicated) to give direction and vision to a ministry." Thus every ministry needs to develop a strategy. The more concise the strategy is, the easier it will be to communicate to church leaders and members as well as to the leaders and workers in your kids ministry. A strategy is essential for all involved to understand and achieve the vision of the ministry.

Your ministry needs a focus, and a strong kids ministry strategy will give you that focus. Your leaders and parents will need to see and understand your focus if they are to be willing to invest their time, talents, and children in your ministry. Without a strategy, the work it takes to fulfill your responsibility can become routine, boring, and, at worst, ineffective. If you are focusing only on your week-by-week tasks, frustration and burnout are real possibilities. With a strategy, the daily or weekly routine becomes important. Strategy helps relate the small tasks to the larger, overarching purpose.

## Is my strategy biblically based?

Everything in life that relates to Kingdom strategy needs to be based on biblical truth. What a minister believes about children and conversion should be based on what the Bible teaches. What a teacher believes and places in practice about guiding behavior should be biblically based. The point: all aspects of kids ministry should be based on biblical principles. In Proverbs 29:18a the Bible states: "Without revelation people run wild" or "Where there is no vision, the people will perish" (KJV).

## Should my ministry strategy be mine alone or one embraced by others?

The most effective plans for ministry are ones that are developed by the key leader of a ministry in cooperation with the leaders and the workers in the ministry. Gather those involved in your kids ministry (teachers, parents, and concerned church members) and allow them to brainstorm the elements for your church's kids ministry strategy.

## What elements should an effective strategy include?

Many churches may want to check out the core objectives in LifeWay's *Levels of Biblical Learning*™ to see what a well-rounded strategy includes. Consider some of the following:

- **What does our church believe about the Bible?** What place do we want the Bible to have in the kids ministry curriculum we choose? What place do kids have in our childhood strategy? Will the curriculum we select be child-centered or teacher-centered? In other words, will the curriculum revolve around what's easiest and sometimes effortless for teachers, or will the happiness and involvement of children be the main consideration in choosing curriculum and ministry emphasis?
- **What does our church believe about teachers?** Should teachers be called to teach children? Do teachers need training, and is our church willing to invest time and money in quality training? What will be the ratio of teachers to children? Will the church be willing to put into place necessary screening procedures in the selection of teachers to provide for the children's safety?
- **Does our church truly believe that parents are the primary spiritual teachers of children?** If this fact is endorsed and embraced, will parent education become a priority in our church's kids ministry and budget? Will parents have input into the type of training they want and need? Will the church family be bold enough to challenge parents to be their children's primary teachers and offer training, mentoring, and tools needed for parents to play this role?

## How do I communicate my strategy?

On a regular basis, gently remind the church family, parents, and teachers about the goals and strategy of childhood ministry. Print and distribute policy and information booklets or brochures. Make video and CD recordings that interestingly state and explain the church's strategy for the kids ministry. Send e-mail blasts with exciting graphics to keep this strategy in front of childhood leadership and parents. Also, post the information under the childhood ministry portion of the church's Web site.

## How do I evaluate my ministry?

Evaluation is needed in all areas of life: physical growth and nutrition, financial goals and achievements, and family health to name a few. When it comes to ministry, consider measuring several areas:

- ➤ How many children are enrolled and what is the average attendance? Is there a pattern of growth?
- ➤ Does the curriculum used for Bible study, discipleship, and special events ensure the teaching of foundational biblical concepts repeatedly during the childhood years?
- ➤ Is there a commitment to a "LifeSpan Spiritual Development Plan" that includes age-suitable Bible teaching and discovery at all ages?
- ➤ Are the efforts in outreach and ministry well-organized and effective?
- ➤ Is training offered for teachers and parents?
- ➤ Are opportunities provided for teachers to be involved in adult Bible study?

## What are annual ministry goals?

Annual ministry goals are derived from your overall strategy and your vision statement. These goals include any program, activity, or event that you will plan in the upcoming budget year. These ministry goals should fall within the boundaries of the strategy. If any goal does not, the question needs to be asked: "Should we really do this?"

## Sample strategy statements:

- ➤ We will seek to minister to the whole child—physically, mentally, socially, emotionally, and spiritually.
- ➤ We will provide age-appropriate Bible study and activities for kids.
- ➤ We will seek to reach unchurched families in our community.
- ➤ We will provide the best programs and events that glorify God.
- ➤ We will seek to provide an environment that guides kids to a lasting relationship with God.
- ➤ We will partner with parents, supporting them as each child's primary spiritual teachers.
- ➤ We will teach children in the ways that God has gifted them to learn.

## Examples of annual ministry goals:

- ➤ Provide on-going Bible study opportunities through Sunday School, discipleship, missions, and music.
- ➤ Plan Vacation Bible School for five days in June. Seek to increase attendance by 20 percent.
- ➤ Plan a community-wide fall festival October 31 as an outreach event.
- ➤ Increase Sunday School attendance by 15 percent.

- Enlist outreach/evangelism teams to follow up after Vacation Bible School and other outreach events.
- Provide resources (curriculum, supplies, equipment) for teachers.
- Provide an overnight camp experience for kids in grades 4–6.

## Where does my strategy meet my budget?

The value and priority that a church family places on kids ministry can be determined by looking at the church's budget. All strategies should include opportunities for the church family to invest financially, as well as with talent and time, in the ministry to kids and their families. The foundational years of childhood education are of paramount importance. Churches need to evaluate their financial investment in kids ministry in the same way a family assesses its personal investments. The earlier an investment is made, the more dividends it will provide in the future.

## What is the role of teachers and parents in developing a childhood strategy?

Each church needs to provide a forum at which teachers and parents can give input and help validate and evaluate the church family's strategy for childhood ministry and education.

## What teaching model should my church use?

One major mistake that many churches make is trying to duplicate the kids ministry of another church. The personalities of churches and communities are unique. The kids ministry strategy needs to reflect the community and its needs. A particular teaching model that is successful in one setting will not necessarily be as effective in another church setting. To learn more about outreach see Chapter 29.

## What is the Hear•Know•Do strategy?

The LifeWay Kids' Hear•Know•Do strategy for kids ministry is designed to lay strong biblical foundations in the lives of children for knowing Jesus personally and experiencing a lifetime of growing to be more like Him. The desire is for spiritual growth to continue as kids become teenagers and as teenagers become adults. This LifeSpan Spiritual Development begins as teachers and parents build spiritual foundations by guiding kids to hear, know, and do God's Word.

- **The first foundational element in a child's spiritual growth is hearing.** As kids learn to trust parents and teachers, they listen to and hear God's Word. The Bible states that the first step toward faith in Jesus is hearing: "So faith comes from what is heard, and what is heard comes through the message about Christ" (Romans 10:17).

- **Kids hear God's Word when they ...**
  - hear foundational Bible stories;
  - hear foundational Bible truths;
  - hear Bible verses;
  - hear Bible story conversation; and
  - hear and sing Bible-related songs.

- **The second foundational element in a child's spiritual growth is knowing God's Word.** Kids begin to know God's Word as they comprehend biblical concepts. For children, knowing God's Word is more than memorization. It is also learning and understanding the meanings of Bible stories, Bible verses, and Bible truths that build foundations for salvation. Paul reminded Timothy: "Continue in what you have learned and firmly believed, knowing those from whom you learned, and that from childhood you have known the sacred Scriptures, which are able to instruct you for salvation through faith in Christ Jesus" (2 Timothy 3:14-15).
  Kids learn and know God's Word when they:
  - hear God's Word;
  - learn foundational Bible stories;
  - learn Bible verses;
  - engage in hands-on Bible-learning games and activities; and
  - participate in large and small group experiences.

- **The third foundational element in a child's spiritual growth is doing God's Word.** While hearing and knowing are foundational to kids' spiritual growth, we must encourage kids to apply God's Word to their everyday lives. Kids exhibit a personal understanding of Bible truths as they do God's Word. This personal knowledge includes using Bible skills and becoming involved in ministry. The Bible states: "Be doers of the word and not hearers only, deceiving yourselves" (James 1:22). As teachers, we help kids do what God's Word says when we:
  - model obedience ourselves;
  - create teaching experiences that imitate everyday experiences;
  - guide discovery learning; and
  - encourage and acknowledge life application.

## What is the *Levels of Biblical Learning*™?

LifeWay's *Levels of Biblical Learning*™ undergirds the Hear•Know•Do strategy and provides visible milestones for the spiritual development of children from babies through preteens across ten biblical concept areas: God, Jesus, Bible, Creation, Family, Self, Church, Community and World, Holy Spirit, and Salvation.

A church that adopts the Hear•Know•Do strategy seeks to create environments that promote spiritual growth in Sunday School, discipleship times, worship experiences, and Vacation Bible School as well as in summer camps and retreats. Churches can come alongside parents and help them be the spiritual leaders for their children that God intended them to be. When churches partner with parents to provide opportunities for kids to hear God's Word (Romans 10:14-17), know God's Word as they understand and comprehend biblical concepts (2 Timothy 3:14-15), and do God's Word by applying it to their everyday lives (James 1:22-25), kids will discover foundational Bible truths that can lead them toward knowing Christ and growing in a lifelong relationship with Him. In all we do, our job is to provide opportunities for kids to hear God's Word, to know God's Word, and to do God's Word by applying it to their lives. We will provide kids with a foundation for knowing Jesus personally and developing a lifelong experience of growing like Him.

Children who have participated in a Hear•Know•Do focused kids ministry should be equipped with the Bible knowledge, Bible skills, and application of biblical truth that will help them successfully transition into the student ministry with a strong spiritual foundation while growing toward adulthood.

*Jerry Vogel and Landry R. Holmes*

*For more information to help in developing a strategy for kids ministry, check out the following items on the Kids Ministry 101 CD-ROM:*
        "LifeSpan Spiritual Development," Item 1
        "Levels of Biblical Learning," Item 2
        "Levels of Bible Skills," Item 3
        "Kids Ministry Strategy," Item 4

# Chapter 3

# What Does a Healthy Kids Ministry Look Like?

A healthy kids ministry strives to meet the physical, mental, emotional, social, and most importantly, the spiritual needs of both kids and teachers. Achieving balance in all these areas can be an overwhelming task, but in the end it is one of the most rewarding in your ministry.

### How do I know whether or not I have a healthy ministry?
Take the time with key leadership and evaluate your ministry in the following areas:

### How do I know that I am meeting the kids' needs?
- Does each area of ministry consider the developmental needs of the child (birth–sixth grade)?
- Are preschoolers and children grouped according to ages and stages of development?
- Is the church aware of the importance of the kids ministry?
- Are leaders aware of the interests and needs of each child?
- Are leaders alert to the unique family situation of each child?
- Are accurate records kept for each child? (attendance, information on family, and health concerns)
- Are efforts made to include kids with special needs?
- Does each child feel welcome?
- Do teachers arrive early to have the room ready and to receive children when they arrive?
- Do teachers call each child by name?
- Do parents know how to use your security system and understand that their children will be released only to the designated adult?
- Are there organized plans for the child each time she is at church?
- Do you provide valuable worship experiences for kids in congregational and/or kids worship?
- Do you have printed preschool and children's policies that communicate efforts to keep the church environment safe and secure?

## How do I know I have effective teaching?

How are you working with your church to find qualified and committed teachers for preschoolers and children?

> - Have you established policies regarding background checks and qualifications?
> - Are job descriptions provided for all leaders?
> - Are there at least two teachers in every classroom?
> - Are teachers involved in training events?
> - Are regular planning meetings with teachers a priority?
> - Are you involved with teachers in outreach and ministry to preschoolers, children, and their families?
> - What are you doing for teacher appreciation?
> - Are you keeping teachers informed of issues and other church activities that may relate to them?

## How do I ensure a safe environment?

- Are the rooms clearly labeled and conveniently located?
- Are the rooms free of clutter and furnished with suggested age-appropriate equipment?
- Are the rooms well-lighted and free of hazards?
- Are the floors and walls clean and attractive?

## How do I equip my teachers?

- Is your curriculum activity-oriented, Bible-based, and child-centered?
- Does the curriculum support the ten foundational concept areas: God, Jesus, Bible, Creation, Family, Self, Church, Community and World, Holy Spirit, and Salvation?
- Are you taking time to become familiar with the curriculum materials to interpret them effectively to your leaders?
- Are resources and materials easily accessible in a central location?
- Does your budget provide for maintaining and improving preschool and children's resources?

*Janet Hamm Williams and Jan Marler*

*For a more in-depth survey to evaluate your kids ministry,
check out the following item on the Kids Ministry 101 CD-ROM:
"Kids Ministry Checklist," Item 5*

# Implementation?

## How do I keep my ducks in a row when I can't even find them?

I began my new calling as Minister of Childhood Education at a church in Mississippi. Even though I was seminary trained, I remember sitting at my desk that first day and asking myself, "Where do I begin? How do I choose the right curriculum for my church? How do I reach families? How do I plan a special event? How do I have an effective leadership meeting? How do I plan a ministry budget, especially when there is so little money?" Through the years I have continued to raise these and other questions about developing, organizing, and administrating a well-rounded kids ministry.

*Cindy Lumpkin*

Set an example of good works yourself, with integrity and dignity in your teaching. Your message is to be sound beyond reproach.

**Titus 2:7-8a**

# Chapter 4
# What Is My Job?

*Acquire wisdom—how much better it is than gold! And acquire understanding—it is preferable to silver. Proverbs 16:16*

What does a kids minister do? Wow … that's a tough question. Many might answer by asking: "What does a kids minister *not* do?" It may seem that you do everything, and more often than not, you are called on to do just about anything; but that's all part of ministry. Being available to do whatever needs to be done is that infamous *#13* on the job description: *other duties as assigned.*

There are, however, a few points that can become the core of a kids minister's job and serve as the basis on which a specific church can build.

- **Be a growing Christian.** When leading a ministry to boys and girls, growing in your relationship with Christ is important. All too often, you don't find yourself on the receiving end of Bible study and daily fellowship with God. The best leader is one who depends on God to lead the way. Find time to be involved in Bible study and personal time with God.
- **Be a team player.** Support the overall ministry of the church. The church's mission isn't just preschoolers, children, and preteens. While understanding your limits, it is important that you support the total work and mission of the church. Don't get shortsighted. Work hard to be a part of other ministries. Show, by example, the attitude you want others to have about the total ministry.
- **Develop and administer a comprehensive ministry plan for childhood ministry.** If you don't have a plan, you'll really never go anywhere. Ask this question: "At the end of a child's journey through the kids ministry of our church, what do I want that child to look like spiritually?" Then ask: "What do I need to do to get him there?" While every church is unique and will have different ideas regarding the programming it offers kids, the childhood minister is responsible for developing a comprehensive ministry plan. This plan will undergird the work and overall mission of the church while seeking to systematically lay spiritual foundations in the lives of the kids it

touches. As the leader of kids ministry, it's your job to prayerfully consider all options and find the best mix of programs and activities that will lead children to a growing relationship with the Savior.

- **Be the team leader for kids ministry.** You really can't (and perhaps shouldn't) do everything yourself. Develop leaders and surround yourself with a team that will get the work done. If there's something that someone else can do, let him or her do it. Check out the giftedness of church members and connect ministry opportunities with those whom God has prepared and gifted to get the job done. Don't confuse delegation with laziness. Work hard to equip the saints to do the work of the church. You're the leader! Lead your team!

- **Equip parents to be the spiritual leaders of their children.** If you really want to make a difference in a child's life, start with the parents. Parents are the most influential people in a child's life. Offer opportunities that will equip parents to fulfill their God-given roles as spiritual leaders and mentors. Offer parent skills classes and tips, parent support groups, and parent training on spiritual issues such as conversion, the Lord's Supper, and baptism. Investing your time in parents will be one of your greatest payoffs.

- **Specific duties as assigned.** Each church will offer programs that reflect the mission and values of that church. Some specific programs you might be called on to oversee include the following: small-group Bible studies (Sunday School), discipleship studies (including Bible skills training), music programming, missions education, Vacation Bible School, and special seasonal programming (summer, Christmas, Easter, and revivals).

Your role as a kids minister is not defined as baby-sitter or cruise director. Your responsibilities might include programming while parents are in adult classes. And yes, entertaining-type events can sometimes be used as tools to accomplish your overall goals. However, your primary role should be as educator, equipper, and encourager for the spiritual development of the kids God has placed in your ministry.

*Bill Emeott*

*For additional information on kids ministry leadership,*
*check out the following items on the Kids Ministry 101 CD-ROM:*
"Leader Job Descriptions for Kids Ministry," Item 6
"Tips for Kids Ministry Leaders," Item 7

# Chapter 5
# How Do I Grow Spiritually and Professionally?

*Trust in the LORD with all your heart, and do not rely on your own understanding; think about Him in all your ways, and He will guide you on the right paths.*
*Proverbs 3:5-6*

You've been on your feet since early morning. You've talked to a multitude—one at a time—and fed all the children under the age of six. You've given hugs and taken diaper bags. You've rounded up substitutes and intercepted children on the run. You've given solace and received criticism. You've planted kisses on babies and reaped gratitude from moms and dads. You've stomped out brush fires and smoothed over irritations. You've heard the sound of music in the sanctuary and sung your own hymns of praise for a child who heard God's call.

What a day! For folks who work with kids, Sunday is a work day— a day for teaching children, caring for children, praying for children, and encouraging parents and teachers. But wait. What about your own encouragement and worship? What about your own spiritual feeding? When do you hear God's Word and receive His guidance?

## What can I do to grow spiritually?

- **Begin with prayer.** Ask God to show you His plan for your spiritual growth. Call out to Him and He will answer. Isaiah tells us about God's response to our prayers: "Even before they call, I will answer; while they are still speaking, I will hear" (Isaiah 65:24). Remember that His plans for you are good (Jeremiah 29:11), and He desires for you to worship Him and grow in His grace. Ask Him how to do it.
- **Set aside a time to listen to God.** Go to your sacred place, wherever that is, the place where you meet God and talk with Him. Take your Bible, a pad, and a pen, and go to that place and listen to God. Don't hurry. Read the Psalm that you always read when you're frazzled. Read it again and wait. As you wait, think through your daily schedule. When can you carve out 30 minutes each day to be alone with God? Covenant with God to meet Him at that time every day.

- **Keep your covenant time with God every day.** Make Bible study and prayer part of your 30 minutes with God. Work on a specific Bible study written by a favorite author, or use an online concordance to find specific verses related to your needs. Whatever you do, read the Word. Talk with God. Write your prayers in a journal or get on your knees before Him. Talk to Him and share your life with Him.
- **Worship God.** The kids ministry will run without you for one hour. Cover whatever bases you need covered. You've enlisted good folks. Trust them to do the work they've been called to do, and then worship. Praise God through music. Hear the Word preached. Let God speak to your heart and give Him praise. You were created to praise Him, not just to serve Him.

## How do I keep up with what's new in kids ministry?

Keeping up with the latest and greatest ideas in kids ministry is critical to your personal ministry. As you read what other churches are doing and what educators are saying about teaching kids, you gain new insights and ideas for your ministry.

- **Read.** Look for new books that can help you gather new ideas on a variety of topics related to kids ministry:
  - ➤ the church's ministry to kids
  - ➤ religious education of kids
  - ➤ teaching kids
  - ➤ working with parents
  - ➤ discipline
  - ➤ special needs
  - ➤ characteristics of the current generation of kids
  - ➤ using creative arts and games
- **Attend kids conferences.** A three- to five-day conference can give you a renewed dedication to your calling, new expertise in an aspect of kids ministry, new friends and networks to draw from, and even a new appreciation for your church.
- **Don't be afraid to try something new.** If you've never planned a stroller, tricycle, and bicycle night for families with young children, try it. You may find new prospects for your church, and it might be a great experience. All you need is a parking lot, food to eat, and games kids and parents can do with 'wheeled vehicles.' Don't be afraid to try some of the ideas you read about in books or hear about in conferences. Take a chance on something new, and it might be just what the kids and families in your church need to connect to one another and to reach out to others in the community.

## How can I avoid burnout?

- **Follow the previously mentioned steps.** Your relationship with God is your lifeline. When you feel those first hints of burnout—run, don't walk, to your sacred place. Get on your knees and rekindle your love for God. Hear Him and follow His plans.
- **Do something that has nothing to do with kids ministry.** If you like to read books, read. If you work out, lift weights. If you play sports, play. If you knit or sew, stitch. If you scrapbook, paste and cut. Whatever you do, make it a part of your week. You need a time to relax and time to let your mind rejuvenate.
- **Exercise.** Now that's a word no one wants to think about! Exercise is a great stress-reliever. This is another burnout buster that takes time, but it is time well spent. Thirty minutes three times a week at the YMCA or your local gym can make a difference in your outlook and your clothing size. If that's not an option, take a walk. Walking and praying are a great way to start or finish your day.
- **Talk with a friend.** Everyone needs a best friend, someone who will love you even when you call with a "full head of steam" and a need to vent. A close friend will pray with and for you, encourage and help you, and listen and counsel you.

## What's integrity got to do with my role at church?

A wise man once said, integrity is holding on to whatever is holding on to you. He made that statement during a sermon on Job. God was holding on to Job, and even with all his trials, Job held on to God. Job was a man of integrity because he knew God was His Redeemer.

On occasion in your role at church, you may be asked to do something that goes against what you believe is best for the kids in your church. How can you maintain your integrity in those times?

- **First,** talk with your senior pastor. If he has made the request, listen to him to learn why he thinks your church needs a specific new program. Hear his reasons for suggesting the program.
- **Second,** ask for time to time to research the program. Find out about the program: Who is publishing it? What is the purpose? What is the cost? How would it fit into your budget? How many volunteers will it need? What type of training will be provided? What do you see positive about it? What do you see negative? How will it fit into your overall vision for the preschoolers and children in your church? Are there other programs you believe would work as well, achieve the same results, and you would feel good about directing?

- **Third,** go back to your pastor with your research and your recommendation. If you have decided that you can direct the program and maintain your integrity, then explain how you will direct the program and how you see it fitting into the vision for the kids ministry of the church. If you really believe the program will not fit into the vision, ask the pastor if you can recommend a different program that will achieve the results he wants.
- **Fourth,** return once more to the pastor with your plans. If he agrees to them, thank him and get to work. If he disagrees, implement the program he prefers and ask God to help you do it. If you feel you cannot implement the program, go back to your sacred place and ask God to help you.

In his second epistle, Peter urged the first-century Christians to: "Grow in the grace and knowledge of our Lord and Savior Jesus Christ" (2 Peter 3:18). Can you accept that admonition as your own? As a Christian and as someone who loves and ministers to kids, growing "in the grace and knowledge of our Lord and Savior Jesus Christ" is the best  personal development plan.

*Judy H. Latham*

# Chapter 6
# How Do I Relate to Church Staff?

*Therefore, my dear brothers, be steadfast, immovable, always excelling in the Lord's work, knowing that your labor in the Lord is not in vain.*
*1 Corinthians 15:58*

We live in a child-focused society, and the successful church is the one that makes sure the kids ministry comes first. Often it is the kids ministry that is responsible for more families coming to know Christ than any other ministry. Communicating effectively with the staff is critical to the success of your ministry.

## How can I convey to the staff the importance of kids ministry?

- **Lead and manage, but above all lead.** Good managers do things right; good leaders do the right things. Develop a positive spirit. You are in a life-changing ministry. A positive spirit communicates to the staff just what kind of minister you are.
- **Be vulnerable.** You do not have all the answers. I know you wish you did. But you do have a direction from God. If you don't have that direction, stop now and ask God to give it to you.
- **Share the vision.**
  - ➤ Vision inspires enthusiasm. Like Isaiah in the temple and Paul on the road to Damascus, share your vision from God with others. Be enthusiastic and excited about what God is doing.
  - ➤ Vision inspires tenacity. Caution! The more you change your vision, the harder it is to communicate it. Be consistent. If this week you are copying a large church's kids ministry and in six months you find another church to copy, then your vision might be from someone else and not from God. Stick with the vision God gave you for your church.
  - ➤ Vision invites, unites, and rallies good people. Work and surround yourself with positive people, and avoid negative people. When you have found the people God has called to this ministry, provide training for them. Your leaders need to be trained to do a better job of ministry. When the other staff members know of the excellence you demand of your leaders, they will listen and respect your ministry even more.

- Vision initiates an inner conversation with God. God is always speaking to you about the vision. Give time every day for God to speak to you and for you to speak to Him.
- Vision enables greatness. It makes space for God in your life.
- Vision helps you stay focused on the greater cause.

- **Attitude is everything.** Your attitude as a kids ministry leader must be, "If we are going to do children's ministry, then we will do it right." The "woe is me" attitude won't cut it anymore. Today many leaders have a "short cut" or "easy way out" attitude. Just because the material is "easier" does not mean it is better. Stand up for what is right. Be consistent and use a Bible study curriculum that is biblically sound and age-appropriate. Forget compromise. Pursue excellence. Kids are worth the extra effort and time required to achieve excellence in Bible study teaching.

- **Give away the praise.** Praise all members of the staff. Make phone calls and send e-mails or cards by regular mail to communicate that you care about them and their ministries. Compliment them instead of competing with them.

- **Offer positive solutions not excuses.** Lots of people will tell you why something won't work. You tell them how it will work. Do your homework. Be up-to-date with the latest research and trends in children's ministry, but create your own ministry.

- **Be a team player.** The winning team is a group of interdependent people who cooperate to achieve a common goal. When the youth ministry is having a car wash, offer to supply snacks from the children's ministry. Then enlist some of your workers to help by cooking and serving the snacks.

- **Write it down.** Write a note to the senior pastor to let him know about the great things going on in your ministry. Put the note under his door, on his desk, or on his e-mail. The result: your pastor will eventually look forward to seeing these positive notes of success from the Sunday experience. Your objective is to leave a high expectation that your church can do the job together with God's help.

- **Be confident before God.** God called you to this ministry, so give Him your best. TRAIN, TRAIN, TRAIN. If you ever get to the place where you think you already know it all, then you are doomed to fail. Always be learning about how to make your ministry the best.

- **Check your image.** Dress and appearance is critical. Look professional while working hard.

*Ken Marler*

# Chapter 7
# How Do I Build a Ministry Team?

*Iron sharpens iron, and one man sharpens another. Proverbs 27:17*

For years, childhood ministry has been accomplished through teams. Each Sunday School class and group in discipleship ministry, missions education, and music education all have two or more teachers carrying out their responsibilities together. They have a deep sense of calling to glorify God through their teaching ministries. The teachers are sanctioned by and accountable to their churches. They are passionate about introducing boys and girls and their parents to Jesus Christ in age-appropriate ways. However, today's churchwide team concept brings a whole new dimension to the ways small groups of member ministers relate to one another when they teach boys and girls.

## What are a ministry team, committee, leadership community, and minister member?

- **Ministry Team:** a group of persons sanctioned by and accountable to a church who are committed to involvement in a specific ministry area to which they have been called.
- **Committee:** a group of persons assigned specific tasks by the church to assist in matters of policy and procedures.
- **Leadership Community:** a group of leaders of various teams who lead the larger group toward a common vision, specific performance goals, and a plan of action.
- **Member Ministers:** All believers are ministers gifted by God.

Let's consider how teams enable our leaders and teachers to serve together in the same direction and produce Kingdom results. As you and your key leaders consider a team ministry approach, pray for God's guidance and wisdom in applying these ideas to your church family.

## What are the implications for leaders of leaders?

Traditionally, we have called a representative group of ministry leaders a council. However, what is the current concept of a council? For many, it is the city council that televises their meetings one night a week. They usually sit behind a large podium and work through readings and regulations to make decisions. Fortunately, that is not what churches do.

With the potential misunderstanding and baggage that the word carries today, many churches are using new terminology such as leadership team or community.

**Community** expresses the intent that through our relationships we are going to carry out our responsibilities. Leaders are not going to serve their teachers all by themselves. They learn from each other, enjoy the fellowship, and share their challenges and victories.

The leader of the leadership community plays an important part in assuring that the community experience is productive. As the leader, do the following for those you lead:
> - Listen to them.
> - Coach them.
> - Set an example.
> - Act accountable and expect them to be accountable.
> - Delegate responsibilities to them according to their strengths, gifts, experiences, abilities, and passions.
> - Carry out your own responsibilities.
> - Develop relationships that foster a culture of love and joy.

In order for the leadership community to experience love and joy, the members of a productive leadership community also play a significant role. They do the following:
> - Accept responsibilities with full knowledge of the purpose and vision of the ministry community.
> - Actively participate in developing relationships through open communication, appreciation, and support with others.
> - Listen to one another and accept the differing opinions.
> - Enable productive teaching teams.
> - Relax and just have fun together.

## What are the implications for teachers?

All kids ministries are comprised of teaching teams. They are the heart of our kids ministries. However, how intentional are you in building strong teaching teams?

The success of teaching teams is greatly enhanced by the team leaders. An increasing number of churches are analyzing personality types before they involve volunteers as lead teachers or department directors. Team leaders need to be able to foster relationships among team members and to encourage teachers to develop their skills. They also need to challenge teachers and themselves to serve with diligence to provide excellent Bible learning opportunities for boys and girls.

## Levels of Leaders and Teachers

- **Emerging**—those who have accepted the fact that God calls all believers to serve Him through ministry.
- **Potential**—those who have agreed to pursue God's calling and direction for their lives in ministry.
- **New**—those who have made a commitment to a particular ministry opportunity.
- **Experienced**—those who have one or more years of experience in a specific ministry.

All of your efforts toward building strong teaching teams have many payoffs. Not only will boys and girls gain more from their learning experiences, the teachers themselves will experience personal growth and a sense of accomplishing something significant for Jesus Christ. Your life will be more satisfying because of decreased stress resulting from productive teaching teams.

Imagine what your life would be like if you had a waiting list of teachers. Feels really good, doesn't it? That dream can become a reality!

### How do I involve members in ministry?
Instead of arm-twisting and begging people to teach, consider a church culture that invites people to join in shared ministry. Churches are using the following actions to involve their members in teaching ministry:

- A churchwide **disciple making process** that leads adults to spiritual growth marked by service;
- A churchwide **mobilization process** that guides member ministers to discover their personal spiritual gifts, passions, and skills; to work with a coach to develop their life mission; and to find God's place for them to serve;
- Churchwide **emphasis on believers** being called to ministry according to their spiritual gifts, special sermons on service, posters in the hallways, brochures about ministries, and a ministry fair;
- **Small-group studies** focused on God's purpose and ministry for their lives; and
- **Spiritual gift inventory** that helps members discover their gifts and plug into ministries where they will utilize their gifts.

## How do I help my leaders develop ministry skills?

Skill development is a journey as the individual teacher develops his or her understandings and skills needed for ministry. The following suggestions can move your ministry toward effectiveness by starting with the individual teacher:

> - **Identify skills** needed by specific leadership and/or teaching roles.
> - **Plan a variety of avenues** for helping teachers develop these skills throughout the year. These avenues must be planned at various levels because skills of new teachers differ from those of experienced teachers.
> - **Participate in the Christian Growth Study Plan (CGSP),** a free service to help churches in the areas of faith and skill development. Certificate plans are available for preschool and children's teachers in Sunday School, discipleship ministry, music education, and missions education. For more information about this tool, go to *www.lifeway.com/cgsp*.
> - **Implement a credentials plan** for potential leaders. When a potential leader has an interest in an age group ministry, he completes that age group's certificate plan in the CGSP. Then he serves as an apprentice with an experienced teacher for a year. At the end of that year, the church will decide if he will become a new leader.

## What are some ways to continue the learning experiences of new leaders?

> - **Develop a mentoring program** in which new teachers ask experienced teachers to become their mentors for a specific time.
> - **Schedule regular planning or team meetings** which include a scheduled time segment for training.
> - **Plan special skill development classes** for new leaders invite them to read a skill book together. When they meet, they reflect on what they read at home.
> - **Associational, state, and national conferences** are fun opportunities for new leaders to develop their skills.
> - **Plan team meetings and conference formats** with experienced teachers as leaders.
> - **Use a Leader-in-Training Plan** through your church library and the CGSP certificate plans.

## How do I encourage spiritual transformation?

Encourage leaders to develop their relationship with Jesus Christ and experience the disciplines of faith through ...

> - small-group Bible study and reflection,
> - worship opportunities to encounter God both corporately and individually, and
> - daily quiet times for prayer and worship.

## How do I show my leaders that I care?

How many times have potential teachers refused to teach because they did not want to lose the ministry of their adult classes? Answer that response by meeting the concerns of recognition, accomplishment, and appreciation in the following caring actions:

> - Connect every teacher to an adult Sunday School class;
> - Encourage adult classes to include associate members in fellowship and ministry events;
> - Present the Christian Growth Study Plan certificates in a meaningful way;
> - Write thank-you notes and birthday cards to individual leaders; and
> - Coordinate food and other ministry actions to teachers who experience crises.

## Which is it—pretend, dream, or reality?

Consider these results of being intentional with childhood ministry teams:

> - Increased participation in teaching ministries because members are attracted to activities that connect them to other people;
> - Change in attitude from one of "I can't find teachers" (scarcity) to an attitude of abundance—"We have more teachers than we need";
> - An opportunity to show the church family how team work is done;
> - An increase in the percentage of happy teachers; and
> - Your church family becomes a launching pad for men and women to engage the use of their spiritual gifts, talents, experiences, and passions to serve Jesus Christ.

## Who should be a part of the kids ministry team?

The kids ministry team oversees the overall ministry programs, plans special events, and sets and implements policies and procedures. This team should include the following people:

> - children and preschool Sunday School team leaders (coordinators, division directors)
> - ETC (Extended Teaching Care) team leader (coordinator, director)

- missions education team leader (coordinator, director)
- discipleship team leader (coordinator, division director)
- Vacation Bible School team leader
- preschool and children's choir coordinators
- weekday education director (when applicable)
- parent
- resource room coordinator (when applicable)
- Bible drill team leader
- deacon
- minister to children (ex-officio)
- minister to preschool (ex-officio)

Each team leader in turn will lead the directors and teachers in their respective ministries.

Being unintentional in developing a team approach is the easier route to follow, but is that the obedient route? Simon had such an encounter with Jesus on his fishing boat. According to Luke 5:4-7, Simon used the best fishing practices of his day. Jesus, however, was not satisfied with Simon's results. He told the expert fisherman to throw the net into the deep water. Jesus knew that fish reside in deep water. Simon did throw the net into the deep water and caught so many fish the net tore from the weight. Much to Simon's amazement, he found a new abundance. Jesus gave Simon a reason to be intentional with his fishing methods and later to be intentional about fishing for men.

We are challenged to rethink our methods of working together and to find new tools to build a ministry team. Be intentional and implement strategies that will build a strong team of ministry leaders. Your effective kids ministry will not be just a dream but will become a reality!

*Morlee Maynard*

# Chapter 8
# How Do I Organize My Ministry?

*A wise man will listen and increase his learning, and a discerning man will obtain guidance. Proverbs 1:5*

Is there anyone in kids ministry with extra time on their hands? Since the answer to that question is most likely "no," it becomes even more important that as a leader in kids ministry you organize your efforts to receive maximum results. Organization is a key to success.

## How do I organize my Sunday School?
Sunday School (or small-group Bible study) is the core of any kids ministry. Organizing that vital portion of your ministry can determine the effectiveness of your overall ministry to children and their families. The following are some important tips to consider for maximum results:

- **Develop a Sunday School team.** Help your teachers see themselves as a team. Help them develop a "we're all in this together" attitude. Develop your team atmosphere during division meetings that include team-building opportunities. Work diligently to help your Sunday School leadership see the value of "team."
- **Develop and use a Sunday School organizational chart.** Developing a Sunday School organizational chart will quickly organize your Sunday School. Begin by recruiting volunteers to serve as division directors for your preschool and children's divisions. Allow the division directors to recruit and direct your department directors/lead teachers. Encourage the department directors to recruit and lead their group of teachers. Example organizational chart:

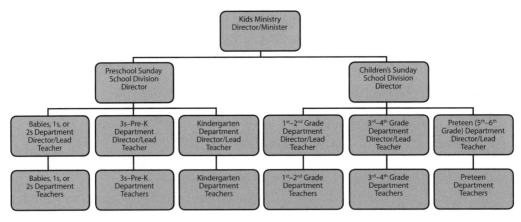

- **Funnel your kids ministry through your Sunday School team.** You've organized your Sunday School ministry. Why not funnel the rest of your kids ministry through this organized, well greased machine? What better way to assimilate a child into the life of the church than with caring teachers who have gotten to know each child on a personal basis? Who better to visit second grade prospects than a second grade teacher? When a family is in need, who better to know those needs than the Sunday School teacher who has already built a relationship with that family? Who better to staff kids seasonal events than the people who work with the groups each week?
- **It's all about relationships.** Relationships built with kids will impact the way they feel about Sunday School, church, and God. Organize your Sunday School through relationships for maximum results.

## How do I organize child care during worship?

Child care, Extended Session, ETC (Extended Teaching Care), or whatever you call it—organizing a volunteer group to teach babies and preschoolers while their parents attend worship—is one of the greatest challenges of preschool ministry. Few have mastered the challenge and many have allowed this responsibility to become the proverbial albatross around the neck of their ministry.

Usually, the majority who serve in this ministry are preschool parents who utilize the service themselves and are assigned to serve on a rotating basis. They serve their time (almost like a sentence or punishment) and look with great anticipation toward the day when their last preschooler moves to "big church" and their service is no longer required.

Take a look at some ideas that may help to turn ETC into an exciting ministry opportunity for you and those with whom you serve:
- **Change your philosophy.** It has often been said, "You get what you ask for!" That's true of child care. If all you want are baby-sitters, then you're probably getting a baby-sitting service. They "check in," (hopefully on time), do the job assigned with little enthusiasm, and then "check out." Not very exciting, but the job gets done. People want to be a part of something that is exciting, valuable, and makes a difference. Change the way you look at child care during worship. Encourage your workers to see child care during worship as an important learning opportunity for the preschoolers who participate.
- **Equip leaders.** Set up your program as an additional teaching opportunity for preschoolers. Why not take advantage of every

chance available to teach boys and girls about God, Jesus, the Bible, and church? Train your child-care teachers and equip them with curriculum and resources that support this ministry philosophy. When you move from baby-sitting to teaching, people are more apt to take child care seriously and make a serious commitment.

- **Use it as an outreach opportunity.** Help your church members see that child care during worship is an outreach tool for reaching young families. Quality child care is high on the priority list of young adults with preschoolers. They need to know that their kids are being well cared for. They are looking for opportunities for their children to learn. Without that assurance, they'll probably not stick around.

- **Enlist the support of the senior leadership,** including the senior pastor. If they see the value, they'll make sure the church understands the value of quality child care during worship. Public support from the senior pastor (both in word and deed) will affect the perception of this ministry and encourage others to participate.

- **It's not just for parents.** Look beyond the list of preschool parents to help staff child care during worship. Many adults are looking for the opportunity to serve in a meaningful way, yet are not prepared to make a standing commitment. Add college students, single adults, and senior adults to your list of possible volunteers.

- **Enlist team captains.** A quick organizational tip for any large ministry program such as child care during worship is to "share the joy!" Recruit team captains to lead teams of child-care teachers on a given week. Determine the frequency your teams will rotate and recruit a captain for each team. These team captains become the leaders for child care during worship on their given Sunday rotation. (Example, a church with eight teams of child-care teachers would have eight team captains. Each team would serve once every eight weeks.) Let leaders know you appreciate them. Everyone wants to know that they are appreciated. Find opportunities to express appreciation to this group of leaders on a regular basis. Those who serve on special occasions (Christmas, Easter, holidays, and special worship services) will need an extra dose of appreciation. Consider ways to express your appreciation. Attention and appreciation go a long way toward consistency with your teams.

## How do I group kids for teaching?

The number of kids in your ministry will determine the age grouping. Smaller churches will group kids with several ages/grades in the same room. Larger churches will have multiple groups of the same age kids.

Consider the following points as you plan to group your kids:

- **Ages.** Group kids according to age. Example: all 2-year-olds together, all first graders together, and all fourth graders together. For smaller numbers of kids you might expand that to first through third graders together, and so forth. Often younger preschoolers are grouped according to stages of development such as crawling or walking.
- **What about kindergartners?** Kindergartners are unique. They are still preschoolers. However, they are technically "in school" and in most school systems they are housed with grade school children. Regardless of where you place kindergartners in your ministry (preschool or children), ensure that age-appropriate curriculum materials and age-suitable surroundings are in place.
- **What about preteens?** The term *preteens* generally refers to kids who are between 10 and 12 years old and are fifth and sixth graders. Many school systems place these kids in middle school. Ideally, preteens at church are best served in an independent preteen ministry, a ministry designed to meet their specific needs. If that is not possible, consider including them in the kids ministry with added responsibilities and special leadership and fellowship opportunities. Placing an 11-year-old child in a ministry with 17- or 18-year-olds can cause concerns for both the preteens and the teenagers. (See Chapter 25 for additional information about preteen ministry.)

### What is the correct ratio of teachers to children and the recommended numbers of children per room?

Always have at least two adults in the room with minor children, regardless of the number of kids attending. There are too many safety possibilities that can occur for one to ignore this standard in ministry: bathroom breaks, accidents requiring a teacher to leave the room, and protection from inappropriate behavior to name a few.

The following ratios are considered best practice for teacher/child ratios and should be considered when staffing your ministry:

| Age of Children | Recommended Teacher/Child Ratio | Maximum Enrollment |
|---|---|---|
| Babies | 1:2 | 12 kids |
| 1s–2s | 1:3 | 12 kids |
| 3s–4s | 1:4 | 16 kids |
| Kindergartners | 1:5 | 20 kids |
| 1st–6th Grades | 1:6 | 24 kids |

## How do I organize multiple ages in one room?

Often, you may find the need to group a broadly-aged range of children together in one classroom. Consider the following helps:

- Add additional teachers to work with specific groupings within the class. This process will allow groups of kids with similar skills to work together simultaneously in the same room.
- Use older kids to partner with younger kids. The buddy system works well when older kids are paired with younger kids to read, write, and complete activities that would otherwise be beyond the younger child's ability.

## How and when do I implement multiple Sunday Schools?

Multiple Sunday Schools are found in churches that, for a variety of reasons, have Sunday Schools at multiple times during the week. Multiple Sunday Schools manifest themselves in a variety of ways. Schedules include:

- Sunday School 1/Worship/Sunday School 2;
- Sunday School and Worship 1 (occurring at the same time) followed by Sunday School and Worship 2 (occurring at the same time);
- Other churches schedule Sunday Schools multiple times throughout the weekend or even throughout the week.

Reasons to consider and implement multiple Sunday Schools:

- Lack of adequate classroom space to accommodate the number of people currently attending.
- Lack of adequate classroom space to accommodate the number of people your church plans to reach.
- Lack of adequate worship space resulting in a need for multiple worship services and adequate Sunday School opportunities to complement the simultaneous worship.
- A desire to meet social and regional needs of those within the community.

Implementing multiple Sunday Schools can be an incredible task. Adding Sunday Schools means the addition of Sunday School leadership. Moving from the traditional one Sunday School to two (or more) Sunday Schools results in doubling (or more) your current leadership. That in itself warrants much prayer and planning before the decision is made to move in that direction. Consider carefully each of the following points when implementing multiple Sunday Schools in your church:

- **Teacher/Child ratios.** Don't water down your desire for quality Bible teaching and relationships by forgoing your teacher/child ratio goals. Work hard to secure adequate leaders. Ask your church leadership (including your pastor) to support your efforts publicly to increase awareness of the need and the desire for the kids in your church to receive the best possible Bible training.
- **Schedule.** The schedule for multiple Sunday Schools is vital for success. Make sure you consider the transition time needed for groups that will meet in the same room.
- **Preschoolers.** When considering multiple Sunday Schools, it is important to remember that space designated for younger preschoolers (those children not yet attending worship) is not doubled. Younger preschoolers do not attend congregational worship but remain in the same classroom the entire time their parents are at church. In fact, many times (with growth) additional space designated to babies, ones, twos, and threes is required.

## What teaching model fits my situation?

Children learn in a variety of ways. Each child is unique and will thrive in a setting that best meets his/her individual needs. As a kids ministry leader, place high value on what is best for the kids in your church.

Consider the following teaching model options:
- **A Traditional Model.** In this model, older preschoolers and children experience both large-group and small-group settings. Elements of a large group might include hearing the Bible story, learning a memory verse, singing a song, working on Bible skills, and praying together. In the traditional model, a small group is designated for application. With lower teacher/child ratios, teachers are able to guide kids to apply Bible truths through a variety of age-appropriate methods in a small group. The emphasis in small group is on building relationships as kids are able to ask questions and teachers are able to guide conversation to reinforce what has been taught in large group.

  In the traditional model, younger preschoolers participate in a variety of Bible-learning activities that utilize Bible conversation, songs, and hands-on learning.

- **The Master Teacher Model.** In this model, one person is designated to be the leader/teacher. This person is responsible for the entire session. He may choose to share the responsibilities (example: a designated song leader or a designated game leader), but ultimately the master teacher leads the bulk of the Bible study. This approach can be especially effective with kids worship, in churches with limited space, or to rally boys and girls for a specific purpose. When choosing this approach, it is important to recruit the right person to be the master teacher. This person must be someone to whom the kids will easily relate and respond. The master teacher becomes responsible for all preparation and must be dedicated to the task.

In large churches, the master teacher approach can place large numbers of kids (who vary in ages/stages) together resulting in the creation of great energy. Occasionally, shy, less active kids become uncomfortable and may even refuse to participate.

In smaller churches, the master teacher approach may be used by default: few kids and few leaders require all the kids in one room with one teacher. While this approach can be exciting and reduce your need for leadership, even in a master teacher setting, good teacher/child ratios are vital for relationship building. For the safety of kids, it is always better to have at least two teachers per class.

- **Rotation Model.** In the rotation model, the same Bible story can be taught for several weeks. During that time, kids are exposed to several methods that teach the Bible story and life application. These methods include drama, movement, crafts, music, or research. In other words, kids rotate through a variety of learning venues that teach or reinforce the same Bible lesson/Bible truth. This model might include a weekly rotation choice or multiple rotations on the same day. Types of rotations might include music, art, computers, cooking, puppets, and drama. These rotations are generally dictated by the curriculum or the expertise of workers in a given church.

A variation on the rotation model allows kids to remain in one classroom with different teachers rotating in for a particular emphasis. This model works well for churches that have space issues and works especially well when using the rotation model with preschoolers.

Some rotation-based curriculum is designed to teach different Bible content each week. Plan to maintain continuity of subject and content so kids don't become confused about the weekly Bible truth and life application.

The rotation model is appealing because it makes recruiting easier. Many people are afraid to make long-time commitments but are open to smaller chunks of time. Many churches use the rotation model to allow leadership to commit to the portion of the week or unit of study that best fits their talents and gifts.

**Our Ultimate Goal:** The opportunity to influence kids is greatest when relationships are developed over time. Much of what kids learn happens as they observe and interact with teachers and other leaders. Any teaching model that does not allow for or promote healthy relationships between leaders and kids is not ideal. As you choose a teaching model, carefully consider your objectives and choose with those goals in mind. Jesus was a Master Teacher, but through His ministry He developed relationships with His disciples and friends that ultimately reached beyond Jerusalem, Judea, and Galilee. His ministry reached the world.

*Bill Emeott*

*For more information on organizing your kids ministry,*
*check out the following items on the Kids Ministry 101 CD-ROM:*
"11 Steps to a Successful Kids Ministry," Item 8
"Kids Ministry in a Small Church," Item 9

# Chapter 9

# What Legal Issues Do I Need to Understand?

*But whoever causes the downfall of one of these little ones who believe in Me—it would be better for him if a heavy millstone were hung around his neck and he were drowned in the depths of the sea! Matthew 18:6*

You don't have to look very far to recognize that the days of assuming everyone means well when it comes to boys and girls is over (if it really ever existed). Keeping kids safe at church has become less and less an assumption and more and more a priority. Below are some questions that you might need to ask yourself, your church family, and even a qualified attorney as you come to grips with the importance of keeping kids safe

## How do I keep children safe at church?

Like anything else that is important, keeping kids safe must become a priority. Setting up standards and guidelines are essential. Start with simple policies like "The Rule of 62." This policy simply means that a person must be an active member of your church for at least six months before being considered for leadership roles with minor children (anyone under the age of 18). Predators won't usually stick around as long as six months. Instead, they move on to an easier target. This rule also states that there will always be at least two adults in any room with minors. This simple rule (policy) is the most effective way to create a safe environment for kids.

Once you have established "The Rule of 62," begin work on more extensive policies and procedures. Involve a team of concerned volunteers to help organize and implement these policies. Whenever possible, include an attorney on your team. Local and state laws are important considerations as you determine what should and should not be included.

While no two churches are the same (different congregations, different programs, different state laws, and so forth), learning what types of security measures for minors other congregations have developed can be helpful. Consider asking churches that already have set policies to share them with you. Do a check on the Internet for reputable ministries that can assist you with standard policies from which to begin your team's work.

Consider the following questions about security policies in churches:

## Should the door of the classroom remain open or closed?

It just depends. When leading minor children at church, it is recommended that leaders stay in plain view. That can be accomplished through appropriately placed windows in the classroom doors or by leaving the doors open. Either way is fine, but always keep in mind that staying above reproach is your best prevention.

## How do I get my church to recognize the need for security policies?

Getting your church members to understand the importance of protection and establishing protection policies is often the hardest part of the whole process. It's not uncommon for people to deny the possibility that something might happen at "their" church. It's much easier to believe that abuse and neglect are issues that others face. Unfortunately, the potential for abuse and neglect of minor children has no barriers and can happen anywhere. One Web site for information on security needs and training is located at *www.ministrysafe.com.*

Education is the key. If you educate your congregation on why one might need to be careful, whom you need to be concerned about, and what specific actions might be considered red flags, you will increase awareness and decrease the chances of children being hurt in your church. Educate your church by sharing statistics and documented cases. Help them to see the value of prevention rather than reaction.

Reiterate the mission of your church. If that mission includes reaching those not yet affiliated with your congregation, then you know that those prospects will desire, and often demand, a sense of security before they enter the life of your church. You are asking parents to entrust you with their most cherished treasures. You should expect that they would want confirmation that their kids are safe. Good, healthy policies and procedures that protect children and give parents a sense of safety equates to good, healthy evangelism.

## How do I prepare volunteer applications?

Volunteer application forms can be helpful in the screening of potential leaders. Check out LifeWay's sample application at *www.lifeway.com/kids* and then ask your church's attorney to help create one designed specifically for your church.

## How do I screen potential (volunteer and paid) teachers?

Approach screening leaders as an interview. Help folks feel at ease by sharing your goals and the ministry description for the leadership position in question. Screening will be easier if you determine that every person who works with minor children will go through the same "interview" process. Never make exceptions to the rule. Then, by using a volunteer application, take the time to "get to know" those who want to work in kids ministry. Follow up on concerns that arise in the application and always check each listed reference. Screening those who work with your children helps prevent discovering later that someone who shouldn't be is working with kids. During the process, you'll get to know your leaders even better.

## How do I do a background check?

Background checks are done through a variety of professional services. One service is online at *www.backgroundchecks.com*. You can also check with your local sheriff's department or contract with a private business.

## How do I handle the information from background checks?

Information discovered through background checks should be confidential and handled with the utmost respect for the person for whom the check was performed and in a manner that will represent your church well. Alarming information should be shared with a senior staff member (in many cases the pastor) and appropriate action taken. If there is any hint of conduct not consistent with your church's policies for working with minors, an additional interview should ensue and a reasonable decision should be made. Occasionally, very tough decisions are necessary. Again, involve the appropriate senior staff member and be united in your decision.

## How do I address accusations of misconduct or abuse?

Each state government has specific, legal obligations for reporting child abuse. This is a very serious matter. Consult with your church's attorney to ensure your church is in compliance with current law.

Consider two additional legal concerns:

## May I copy curriculum?

More and more churches are finding themselves in court defending accusations of "theft by copy!" The illegal copying of curriculum, music, song lyrics, and so forth, is a serious crime against those who would otherwise receive royalties from the proper selling and distribution of their property (their ideas).

In recent years, however, there have been some curricula published with the sole purpose for you to photocopy it to create the desired number you need. The publisher created and priced that resource to ensure that those responsible for its creation are compensated. If you have purchased reproducible curriculum, that information will be clearly stated, and you will clearly understand your rights as a purchaser. The best rule of thumb is not to assume that it is okay to copy. Do your research; ask permission; be an example of honesty and integrity to the kids you teach. Remember, just because you have a copy machine, doesn't make it okay to copy and distribute curriculum.

## May I show movies?

Movies are copyrighted works. Movies which are rented or purchased are for viewing only within the context of a home. Therefore, showing movies without permission is against the law, is a punishable crime, and is not something for your church to do. You can purchase services that allow you to receive a license to show specific, pre-approved releases. Not all movie producers and companies participate in this service. Check with the licensing service to ensure you are acting within the parameters of your agreement. One licensing service is available online at *www.cvli.com*.

## What does all this mean to me?

Policies and procedures are essential to keeping a standard of safety. Don't think it's something you don't need to deal with. It is! Work diligently to protect the reputation of your ministry, your church, and the leaders who serve in your ministry. More importantly, work diligently to protect the boys and girls God has entrusted to your care.

*Bill Emeott*

*For more information on screening volunteers for your kids ministry,
check out the following items on the Kids Ministry 101 CD-ROM:*
"Screening Form," Item 10A
"Release Form," Item 10B

# Chapter 10
# How Do I Enlist and Retain Leaders?

*And He personally gave some to be apostles, some prophets, some evangelists, some pastors and teachers, for the training of the saints in the work of ministry, to build up the body of Christ. Ephesians 4:11-12*

"How do I enlist?" is one of the most frequently asked questions in kids ministry. Larger churches, smaller churches, and every church in between seem to deal with the same question: "How do I find more workers?"

One of the greatest blessings in any family is the blessing of children. That's true of our church families, too. But, with every blessing comes responsibility. As parents, we have a responsibility to nurture and rear our kids. As a church family, we have a similar responsibility. I'm convinced that God has not brought boys and girls into our care without bringing adult leadership to minister to them. The issue is finding, recruiting, and retaining these teams of leaders.

## What steps do I need to take to enlist leadership for my kids ministry that I will be able to retain for years to come?

- **Know that God is in control.** As much as you desire for the boys and girls in your ministry to have good teachers and quality learning experiences, you can trust that God wants that for them even more. Philippians 4:19 teaches that God will supply all your needs. Why would you think that He would forget you when it comes to your need for leadership in this important ministry? Ask, seek, and knock! After all, God is in control.
- **Know a good recruit when you see one.** Before you begin enlisting, know what you're looking for. Kids look up to their leaders; make sure that those you recruit are people who will make strong, positive role models for boys and girls. Some characteristics of a good recruit include the following:
  - **A growing Christian**—Look for men and women who have a growing relationship with God.
  - **An active church member**—Leaders of kids should be active, supportive members of your church.
  - **Called by God**—Nothing can take the place of knowing you are

called by God to lead kids. Seek folks who sense God is leading them to kids ministry.

> **Loves kids**—A no brainer, right? Wrong. Unfortunately, not everyone who works with kids at church truly loves them. Many folks find themselves being persuaded by a plea or somehow guilted into ministry with little concern or a true love for kids and their spiritual well-being. Watch to see those to whom kids naturally gravitate. You'll probably find a recruit who genuinely loves kids.

> **Willing to prepare**—I've not met a curriculum yet that prepares itself. There is a certain amount of preparation that is required whenever you lead kids. Be honest about the required preparation and make sure your recruits are willing to devote time to this important aspect of kids ministry!

> **Willing to be a part of a team**—Kids ministry programming is never a solo act. You will always need multiple leaders working together. Be certain each recruit is a team player, willing to work with the team to carry out the goal.

- **Know how many leaders you need.**
  > Know that staffing church ministries means you should *always* have at least two adults in the room with minor children (anyone under the age of 18). That rule of thumb should never be broken.
  > Move toward a healthy teacher/child ratio in each classroom. A recommended ratio depends on the ages of the children that will be in a particular classroom. For babies there should be 1 adult for every 2 babies (remember our rule of thumb above though). For 1s and 2s: 1 adult for every 3 kids. For 3s and 4s: 1 adult for every 4 kids. Kindergartners: 1 adult for every 5 kids. In grade school the recommended ratio is 1 adult for every 6 kids. (See Chapter 8 for more information about teacher/child ratios).

- **Use a ministry description.** When you approach a possible candidate, be ready with a written ministry description. It shows people you've thought things through. It helps you figure out whom you *really* need in specific positions. It gives you something to give to possible volunteers that they can read before making an honest decision. It gives you something to use in an interview. Yes, an interview. Getting the wrong people in the wrong jobs can lead to endless turnover and additional recruiting. People want to be involved in something that matters. Giving them a ministry description says, "This is important."

- **Don't forget the men.** Men make great leaders with kids. Don't assume that kids ministry is for women only; that's not biblical either. Consider the men who may be called to your area of ministry.

Remember, husbands and wives often make great teaching teams. However, for security they should teach in the same classroom only when there is a third teacher who is not related to either of them.

- **Use the buddy system.** Some leadership roles can look a bit overwhelming. However, if two folks are recruited to fill a particular position as co-leaders, co-teachers, or co-coordinators, the task can look more doable. When recruiting two friends, it might even look fun! Consider recruiting pairs for some jobs. Consider recruiting "first time" teachers with a partner.

- **Share the joy! Jesus let His followers share in recruiting (John 1: 31-51).** Why wouldn't you? As the kids ministry leader, concentrate on recruiting division directors. For every major program/event in your ministry, recruit someone to be in charge of that program or event. That person will then recruit folks who will serve in leadership roles under her. Then those folks will recruit leaders who will serve under them. An example: In a church running 50 kids in Sunday School, the ministry leader (you) should recruit a children's division leader. The division leader will recruit a leader for each class, and the class leaders will recruit the other teachers needed to fulfill a healthy teacher/child ratio. When you approach recruiting in that way, everyone does a little. Together you've completed the job—you've "shared the joy!"

- **Provide training.** There's nothing more frustrating than being asked to do a job and then not being given the tools to do it well. Make sure that you provide training to your team on a regular basis. National, state, local, and even in-house trainings are keys to success, and success means longevity. Explore different options, but keep growing your team.

- **Provide support.** All too often we ask volunteers to fill positions and leave them with little or no support. Drop by to check on new recruits. Make sure they know you're available and want to help them be successful. Schedule regular times (quarterly, monthly, or even weekly) to bring your team together to show your support and allow them to share ideas and concerns that will make the ministry more effective. Creating a sense of team doesn't happen outside of a few huddles/ pep rallies/meetings along the way. Be careful, however, to conduct meetings that are actually helpful. Plan to share something worth hearing and add exciting and fun methods for presenting information. Poorly planned meetings will kill your momentum; worthwhile meetings are essential to building it.

- **Appreciate you leaders.** Everyone wants to feel appreciated, and usually it's the little things that mean the most. Quick notes or an e-mail; a candy gram with a short thank-you note attached; a "teacher of the week" profile on a ministry board; and yes, even the old pat on the back with a sincere thank-you can show your leadership team members how valuable they are and how much you appreciate them. A little affirmation mixed in with a heaping dose of appreciation will go a long way in maintaining a volunteer ministry.
- **Never stop! Always be on the lookout.** If your kids ministry is going to grow, you're going to need additional team members. Be watchful of whom God is bringing into your ministry and expect Him to provide all your needs, "according to His riches in glory in Christ Jesus" (Philippians 4:19).

*Bill Emeott*

*For more information on job descriptions and tips for leaders in your kids ministry, check out the following items on the Kids Ministry 101 CD-ROM:*
"Leader Job Descriptions for Kids Ministry," Item 6
"40 Easy Teacher Appreciation Ideas," Item 11

# Chapter 11

# How Do I Develop Policies and Procedures?

*But everything must be done decently and in order. 1 Corinthians 14:40*

Policies and procedures ensure that your ministry is ready for children and families whenever they come to church. A church must protect itself from any question of negligence and thus help protect its long-term ministry to children, parents, and teachers.

## Why does your church need to provide policies and procedures?

- The children deserve the best possible care.
- The teachers deserve the benefit of using resources and materials that meet the needs of the children they are teaching.
- The church deserves the best opportunity for ministry to the children and their families.
- The parents deserve to know their child is in a safe, secure, and healthy environment where teaching about God is held to a high standard of excellence and integrity.
- The children deserve a place to say, "This is my room where I learn about God."

## How do you get started? Who is involved?

Proverbs 20:18a reads: "Finalize plans through counsel." Seek counsel from several individuals. Form a group to determine the policies and procedures necessary for your church. Invite a mixture of people who have a vested interest in the kids in the church. Possible members of the group:

- health care professional
- involved parents (2)
- legal counsel
- childhood minister
- preschool teacher
- children's teacher
- education director (may come as needed)
- fire marshal or a firefighter (as needed on fire safety issues)
- nurse (as needed on health issues)
- nutritionist (as needed on issues about foods served at church)

A childhood minister, a division director, or a member of the kids ministry team may facilitate the subgroup meeting to make sure the agenda is followed. Members of the group must be ones who can keep confidences and work with a team spirit so that policies and procedures can be formulated. Once the group has agreed on the policies, introduce them to parents and other individuals who would need to be aware of them. Parents and others may want to have input into policies and ask questions regarding specific ones. When parents and others feel their views are considered, they are more likely to follow the guidelines. Some church families even choose to vote to affirm and validate these policies.

## What policies and procedures need to be considered?

Be sure to consider the needs of the kids. When are kids at church? Where are their programs held (such as missions, music, Sunday School, discipleship training, weekday programs, church-wide events)?

> Begin to think of the specific areas that need to be included in the policies and procedures.
> Gather information on each topic.
> Make assignments. Consider dividing the subgroup into teams to gather and write specific guidelines.

Make your policies and procedures specific to meet the individual needs of your preschool (birth–kindergarten) and children's (Grades 1–6) ministries. Expand or include other items that would further protect the church. Consider the location of these ministries in your church facility to the proximity of the street, worship center, adult classrooms, and playground.

Policies might include some legal issues that need to be covered. Make sure that you include these issues in the safety, security, and child abuse sections of the policies and procedures. Consult with your church's lawyer and the liability insurance guidelines from your church's insurance agency.

- **General Policies may include the following types of information:**
  > opening and closing times,
  > procedures for dropping off and picking up children,
  > specific ages of children who are allowed in each classroom,
  > the church's philosophy on the importance of teaching children,
  > the way preschoolers and children are taught at church,
  > the curriculum used for Bible teaching,
  > a minimum of two teachers in each classroom, and
  > specific supplies parents need to bring for babies and 1-year-olds.

- **Playground Policies may include the following:**
  - adult supervision (two adult rule) on the playground;
  - ages of children allowed on the playground;
  - the playground hours, groups using the playground, and so forth;
  - regular audit and inspection of playground equipment;
  - types of equipment on the playground for specific ages; and
  - first aid supplies available to teachers while on the playground (anti-bacterial wipes, band-aids, and disposable gloves).

- **Health Policies may include the following topics:**
  - symptoms that prevent children from coming to church for the protection of all children,
  - procedures for care of a child who becomes ill at church,
  - calling parents when their child becomes ill at church,
  - guidelines for administering medication at church (only parents may administer medication at church), and
  - filling out a child information form to report allergies and other disorders.

- **Infectious Disease Policies may address the following situations:**
  - how the church handles privacy of families who have disclosed a specific disease,
  - how home ministries can be handled for the family and child,
  - how the cleaning of equipment and resources is done within each classroom,
  - consultation with a physician for information regarding a particular infectious disease,
  - specific information to prepare teachers and leaders about these policies, and
  - additional information from the Center for Disease Control (CDC) on infectious diseases.

- **Hygiene Policies may address the following issues:**
  - procedures for cleaning and disinfecting bathrooms, diapering areas, and equipment (¼ cup of bleach to a gallon of water);
  - procedures for cleaning toys and other items used by the children (1 tablespoon of bleach to 1 gallon of water);
  - the regular cleaning of sinks, rest rooms, cabinet tops, mats, and all vinyl equipment in a babies and 1-year-old room;
  - assigning responsibility for cleaning;
  - hand washing procedures;

- hygiene guidelines for teachers;
- hygiene guidelines for children;
- diaper changing procedures;
- body fluid spill guidelines;
- information from the Center for Disease Control (CDC) for up-to-date hygiene practices; and
- classroom cleaning procedures (placing toys, resources, and materials in certain locations following their use in any program).

- **Safety Policies may include guidelines such as the following:**
  - the number of teachers and ages of teachers in each classroom (teachers must be 18-years-old or older, always at least two teachers in every room);
  - the teacher/pupil ratio for each age-group classroom (Chapter 8);
  - designation of age-group classrooms;
  - emergency procedures in case of fire, weather-related issues, power outages, or flooding (a discussion with the local fire marshal will help determine the best exits for each of these emergencies);
  - designated locations for evacuation routes in emergencies (fire, weather-related issues, power outages, or flooding);
  - designated locations for parents to meet children following an emergency;
  - locations of first-aid kits and fire extinguishers;
  - an emergency bag for all classrooms that contains the class roll, first-aid supplies, class sign, and disposable disinfecting cloths;
  - allergy signs for classroom doors anytime foods are tasted, plants are used, and pets are brought in;
  - a location for class rolls that include parent names or designated guardians and phone numbers for easy access;
  - procedures for locating parents when an emergency occurs;
  - policies for reporting any accident;
  - training teachers to complete an accident/incident form in the event of an accident;
  - procedures for warming bottles (use of crock pots instead of microwave ovens);
  - the maintenance of the outdoor and indoor environments such as hallways, sidewalks, steps, parking areas, worship center, and classrooms; and
  - procedures for ensuring equipment in the classrooms and on the playgrounds is in good repair.

- **Security Policies may include the following:**
  - ➤ security procedures for dropping off and picking up children any time they are at church (Sunday School, Weekday Program, music, missions, TeamKID, VBS, and so forth),
  - ➤ communication of the details about the security system (card system, computer check-in, and so forth) in writing to parents,
  - ➤ education of teachers and leaders about the security system and the enforcement of it,
  - ➤ medical release forms and accident report forms along with instructions for use,
  - ➤ information from the custodial parent on how to manage release of children (including gathering information for each child in a separation or divorce situation in order to protect the child and the church),
  - ➤ background checks on all volunteers or employed teachers who work with minors,
  - ➤ consultation with a legal representative to help formulate policies for keeping all background checks confidential and secure,
  - ➤ a teacher's responsibility to create an environment for teaching biblical content to preschoolers and children, and
  - ➤ husbands and wives teaching in the same classroom only when there is a third teacher who is not related to either of them.

- **Child Abuse Policies may include the following:**
  - ➤ setting up training for recognizing child abuse,
  - ➤ developing procedures for reporting child abuse and responding after child abuse has been reported, and
  - ➤ consulting with a lawyer who is familiar with liability law and the church's liability in case of child abuse.

- **Parent Policies might include the following:**
  - ➤ information needed at church, labeling of bottles and diaper bags, and so forth;
  - ➤ information about toys that should be left at home;
  - ➤ use of security procedures;
  - ➤ completion of the sign-in sheet;
  - ➤ procedures for receiving kids after Sunday School or worship;
  - ➤ information about teaching kids about God, Jesus, and the Bible at home; and
  - ➤ procedures for checking on kids during the session.

## How does the research become policy?

- **Meet with the committee to report on the work accomplished toward specific guidelines.** Provide an opportunity for each subgroup to report their policies and procedures. All members of the committee can appreciate the work of each subgroup and give suggestions when needed.

- **As a committee,** come to a consensus about the work completed on specific guidelines. Determine the protocol regarding the acceptance of the policies and procedures. Plan what needs to happen next to make sure that parents and teachers are on board with all that is stated in the policies.

- **Plan the Preschool/Children's Policy Manual.** Consider printing a written policy manual so that everyone can be aware of all policies and procedures. Pull out specific information and print it in a small brochure to give to all parents as well as to visitors and new members.

Most parents will be pleased to see that a church has placed the kids ministries high on their agenda. Revisit your policies from time to time to ensure that information remains current.

*Ann Edwards*

*For more information on health and safety guidelines for your kids ministry, check out the following items on the Kids Ministry 101 CD-ROM:*

"Safety Guidelines," Item 12
"Preschool Room Safety Checklist," Item 13
"Cleaning Surfaces," Item 14
"Cleaning Materials," Item 15
"Washing Hands," Item 16
"Hygiene," Item 17
"Safe and Unsafe Plants," Item 18

# Chapter 12
# What Is a Ministry Budget?

In brainstorming sessions, ideas flow without regard to their practicality and cost. Brainstorming is a good way to help us think outside the box. However, we do not live in a no limits world. One of the realities of kids ministry is that it costs money. Children and preschool leaders are not responsible just for the wise spending of the church's money, but they should also be involved in setting the budget for the kids ministry.

## Why is a budget important?
Money is not the first factor to consider when developing a children's ministry budget. In fact, the dollar signs appear only after the planning process is complete. The following ideas are suggestions for beginning a ministry-based budget planning process:

> - Enlist the help of persons committed to the kids ministry, perhaps a task force or committee. Lead them through the budget process and ask for their input.
> - Know the vision for kids ministry at your church. (Ideally, each church should have a vision statement for its kids ministry.)
> - Decide what programs and activities are needed to fulfill the vision.
> - Develop an annual calendar to include all programs and activities.
> - Set goals for the number of persons that each activity will reach.
> - Determine the leadership needed to accomplish the goals.

Using this information, carefully research the cost. Refer to the church's financial records for the past two years to determine the amount of money spent on various programs and activities. Then look in catalogs and other resources to determine the cost of curriculum and supplies. Inventory the church's current equipment to see what items may need to be repaired or replaced. If necessary, obtain bids from suppliers for these costs.

## How do I develop a budget?

With your church calendar of activities as a guide, develop a budget for each month. Some expenditures are seasonal such as Vacation Bible School. Knowing that Vacation Bible School will be conducted in June, for example, will help you anticipate increased expenses that month. Curriculum costs generally occur once a quarter and should be added in the appropriate months. Computing each month's expenses will enable you to arrive at an accurate total for the year.

Also, keep a record of the expenses for special events. File this information to be used when you plan another similar event and for the next year's budget. For example, after a retreat, itemize and total the cost. Include the following information:

- transportation (rental of vans, gasoline);
- cost of retreat facility;
- food and snacks;
- speaker and other program guests;
- publicity;
- curriculum materials, books, and other materials; and
- adult leaders.

When you begin with a vision for kids ministry, that vision is reflected in a calendar of activities and programs. When you have done your homework researching the costs, the request for money is easier to justify. Do not just look back at last year's budget and automatically ask for the same amount or a percentage increase. Instead, take time each year to go through the process of developing a budget based on the plans for the year. Present it to the proper committees or teams in your church. Defend it with the information you have discovered in your research. Be an advocate for the children and preschoolers in your church and champion the need for adequate funds to accomplish the goals of the ministry.

*Carolle Green*

*For a simple budget worksheet to use in your kids ministry,
check out the following items on the Kids Ministry 101 CD-ROM:
"Kids Ministry Budget Worksheet," Item 19*

# Chapter 13
# Why Should I Market My Ministry?

> To the weak I became weak, in order to win the weak. I have become all things to all people, so that I may by all means save some. 1 Corinthians 9:22

Most kids leaders struggle with how to best "market" their ministry. With small budgets, limited time, and too few volunteers, it's easy to miss some fundamental principles that will ultimately save time and make your ministry more meaningful and successful.

## What am I selling?

A common mistake leaders make is focusing on a product or service. We promote events, plead for volunteers, and beg for equipment and supplies. Try a new approach by marketing how the experience will benefit the kids. Ask yourself: "How can we make the Sunday morning experience more meaningful for children and easier for parents? How can I make the Sunday morning experience positive and memorable?"

## Who am I serving?

Children, parents, and leaders are the main target of your ministry. However, you will also need to target your pastor, church staff, potential leaders, and the finance committee. Make sure to craft each message to the right audience.

## How do I market effectively in the community?

- Determine a target audience. Are you communicating to kids, leaders, parents, or the community? Avoid combining messages.
- Surround yourself with people who think differently from you.
- Know the needs of the children, families, and your community.
- Discover the needs of your community by consulting a demographic study or census results. Include a diversity of people when making decisions about ministry.
- Know the expectation of young families. They are looking for churches that will provide choices and excellence in ministry. They want their needs met in a personal way and desire to receive communications in the way they prefer to receive them.
- Make sure your ministry's Web site is up-to-date and user friendly.

## How do I market my ministry to the pastor and staff?

- Know your pastor's priorities.
- Be a professional. Be positive. Present solutions, not excuses.
- Be prepared to state how kids ministries will support the vision of the church. For example, how do you plan to reach new families? What is your plan for spiritual development of children? How will this plan translate into baptisms? What will it cost? How will you communicate the vision?

## How do I brand my ministry?

Establish your brand by understanding who you are. What attributes does your "brand" (i.e. your ministry) embody? The following is a sample list:

- Strengths—programming, trained leaders, security systems;
- Weaknesses—lack of committed leaders, insufficient budget, limited space and equipment;
- Opportunities—a renovated facility, a new security system, a church-wide focus on leader training; and
- Threats—churches with similar programming, budget shortfalls.

Describe your ministry's desirable attributes. Ask yourself, "What makes our kids ministry different from the church around the corner?" Examples:

- the church's state-of-the-art security system;
- well-trained leaders;
- excellent, age-appropriate curriculum; and
- a quality Christian education for children.

*Remember: Be realistic! DON'T ADVERTISE IT IF YOU CAN'T PROVIDE IT!*

## Why is competitive analysis important?

Consider your direct competition. If a nearby church has scheduled VBS during the same week as yours, ask: "How is our VBS different from theirs? Why would families choose to attend our VBS?" Research indirect competition such as little league tryouts scheduled the same day as your special event. Be flexible and schedule around the competition.

## What is a satisfaction survey?

Ask teachers and parents to complete a satisfaction survey to help you evaluate the effectiveness of your ministry. Sample questions:

- Is our church reaching and ministering to children?
- Do our teachers feel fulfilled in teaching children?
- Are our teachers equipped to teach children?

- Do we have the supplies and equipment that we need?
- How could we better meet the needs of our community?
- Do teachers, parents, and children feel supported both emotionally and spiritually?
- Do we address issues in a timely manner?

## How do I market a special event?

Determine a strategy when planning an event. Why are you providing this event? How will it benefit the attendee? Don't plan an event because you have always had it.

- List the features of the event and determine benefits of the event.
- Enlist a pre-event staff to be responsible for promotion and marketing strategies. Use every available avenue to promote an event. Press releases are a great no-cost way to advertise in newspapers and on local radio and/or television stations.
- Consider the timing of the event. What else is happening in your community on this date? Should you use a theme? What outreach potential would the event provide? Post signs directing attendees to the site location.
- Enlist greeters to answer questions. Be ready early. Instruct volunteers of the importance of speaking to everyone. This is a great time to get to know kids and their families.
- Consider fun ways to register attendees. Door prizes and "guess how many jelly beans are in the jar" kinds of experiences are successful ways to obtain needed information.
- Place signs directed to kids at their eye level.
- Enlist a cleanup crew.
- Contact kids and parents following an event to thank them for attending and to provide additional information regarding the kids ministry at your church.

In today's world, children and their families are bombarded with marketing messages from food choices to what kind of car to drive. Are you willing to use some of the same methods to market your ministry? Your ministry's message is vital, and your ultimate goals are to help children know and follow God and to reach families for Christ.

*Jan Marler*

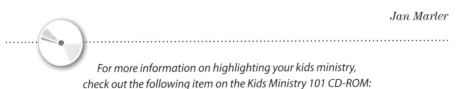

*For more information on highlighting your kids ministry,*
*check out the following item on the Kids Ministry 101 CD-ROM:*
*"ABCs of Getting the Word Out," Item 20*

# Chapter 14
# What Should My Kids Space Look Like?

*Safe, Secure, Sanitary, and Spacious are the four Ss required for kids ministry space.*

One of the most obvious ways we communicate the priority we place on kids ministry is through the physical space assigned to children and other areas of ministry. Providing quality space for kids by making it attractive, functional, fun, and accessible will aid in attracting families to the church. An attractive space also makes your members proud and eager to invite others to church. If the space is inadequate and unappealing, people will hesitate to invite others. They will find themselves apologizing for the space, and the workers will be trying to overcome its deficiencies rather than reaping the benefits of an attractive and functional space.

## What does kids ministry space look like?
*Safe, Secure, Sanitary,* and *Spacious* are the four Ss required of space that works well for kids ministry.

## Is your space safe?
For a building to be safe, adequate exits, lighting, ventilation, and sound structure are essential. Without these basics, the building is not a safe and appropriate place to teach children. Most local fire departments will conduct a free walk-through to point out any problems or potential problems that need to be addressed for fire safety.

Preschool rooms should be on the ground floor. Rest room facilities need to be in or immediately adjacent to each teaching room so that young children do not have to leave the classroom and go down a hall to a rest room. Access to a toilet is most important for those children who are being potty trained and are too young to go to the rest room unsupervised. For older children, rest rooms still need to be in a supervised area near the classrooms and preferably not shared with other age groups.

## Is your space secure?
Today, parents have a heightened awareness of the importance of control over who enters the children's areas. Implementing a security system that designates the person who will pick up each child is a must for a secure

space for Bible study. If possible, position the kids rooms where traffic is limited to workers, children, and parents, especially in the preschool area.

## Is your space sanitary?

Good sanitation is essential to the health of children. Maintaining a clean teaching environment should be a priority of your children's ministry. Hand washing sinks should be in each classroom so workers can wash between diaper changes in younger preschool rooms and for cleanups in all rooms. All objects in younger preschool rooms need to be washable. Rooms need to be tidy; and ceilings, walls, and floors need to be stain-free. Clean rooms are a sign to parents that you are as concerned as they are about the learning environment and good health of their children.

## Is your space spacious?

To conduct kids ministry effectively, you need a certain amount of square footage per child. Two to three times as much space is required to accommodate a child as is needed for an adult. The preschool child needs 35 square feet of floor space, and the grade school child needs 25 square feet for the best teaching and learning to occur. Provide rooms as close to these space requirements as possible. When calculating space, remember to allow room for future growth.

Why so much space? Children need room to explore, and kids rooms require more furniture than adult rooms. In addition to chairs, a kids classroom will have tables, learning centers, bookshelves, sometimes cribs and rockers, storage cabinets, and other items necessary for teaching.

## What are the details I need to consider when I assess my space?

To make sure your preschool and children's space encourages quality teaching and learning, consider the following guidelines:

- **Location**—Assign like age-group classrooms in the same area of the building if possible. The preschool area needs to be located near a convenient entrance, preferably with a covered drop-off area. This allows parents to enter the building, drop off their children, and then proceed to their classrooms. Convenience to parking and the worship area are also important. Avoid a layout that requires people to walk through the preschool and children's areas to get to another part of the building. Also, arrange your space to allow for future expansion.
- **Doors**—Classroom doors should have a small, glass view panel to allow monitoring of classroom activities. Such doors will help assure parents that nothing inappropriate will happen.

- **Light and Lighting**—Numerous studies have demonstrated that natural light has a profound impact on the learning of children. Introduce natural light with ample windows whenever possible. Rooms should also be well-lit for teaching on cloudy days and at night. Fluorescent lights wired to provide options of different levels of lighting are appropriate for most classrooms. Indirect light is great for bed babies. Other kids rooms need the option of dimming lights for napping or when teaching methods call for using media.
- **Colors**—Using appropriate colors in kids spaces can help make the space more exciting and interesting. Too much intense color can aggravate behavioral problems. Too little color results in a boring space. Use soft colors that will not over stimulate.
- **Flooring**—Use flooring that can be cleaned thoroughly. Carpets with thick pads can be a problem because they hold moisture, bacteria, and odors. Removable rugs that can be cleaned or replaced are recommended. A simple composition or vinyl tile is a good basic flooring that is easily cleaned and maintained and is cost effective.

## Should I have themed spaces?

To make an impression on kids and parents, some churches design themed kids spaces. If you have the option, create a reception area and broad hallways. Here, kid-appropriate decorations and even theme-oriented sculptures and professionally painted graphics can attract the attention of children and parents alike. Such artwork will proclaim that this is a kids area, and you believe learning about Jesus and the Bible should be fun!

Three things seem to determine the success of themed spaces: the location, the quality of the work, and the contribution they make to the ministry. If you are considering this kind of investment, consider several factors that can make it a valuable asset to the ministry:
- **Location**—Locate theme-oriented graphics and objects in reception areas and other non-teaching spaces where children, parents, and workers can see and enjoy the artwork. They make a strong first impression and will not distract from the teaching in the classroom. Leave the teaching rooms clear of such artwork to allow teachers to provide focused materials that reinforce their teaching.
- **Quality**—If you decide to provide themed artwork, make the investment to create excellent murals or other graphic images. Anything but the best may be counterproductive to the message of a high quality ministry you want to communicate. Not many churches are blessed with members who are talented artisans. The advantage of

hiring an outside artist to do the work is that you do not have to worry about offending the artist when the artwork becomes outdated or if you are just ready for a change! When artwork gets dirty or marred, it can look worse than a freshly painted plain wall. Before you invest, plan on how you will protect the art from damage and consider how you will repair it if it does get damaged.

- **Subject matter**—The choice of theme(s) for the kids area should be consistent with the biblical messages that are being taught elsewhere in the ministry. The subject matter should not be a confusing mixture of real life and fantasy. This can cause kids to confuse Jesus, Moses, and other real-life persons with fictional characters. A good source for artwork ideas might be Vacation Bible School themes. This would allow you to change your theme each year at VBS time and continue using that theme throughout that year until the next theme makes its debut. Streetscapes and nature themes make good decorations, too. Whether paintings or three-dimensional representations like storefronts, trees, animals, hills, clouds, or stars, these can be an attractive and eye-catching way to let people know you are focused on kids. Very exciting spaces can also utilize fun colors and shapes without the investment in more complex murals. The space can still communicate, "This is the kids zone," and "We have fun here," while becoming a canvas for other decorations, announcements, and temporary artwork without conflicting with a theme.

*Gary Nicholson*

*For more information equipment and space for your kids ministry,
check out the following items on the Kids Ministry 101 CD-ROM:*
"Basic Equipment List," Item 21
"Preschool Educational Space," Item 22
"Children's Educational Space," Item 23

# Chapter 15
# What Do I Do with My Resources?

Resources: Reuse, Recycle, Re-shelve

Admit it! It takes a lot of stuff to teach children. You need glue, paper (all sorts), crayons, markers, toys, a Giant Game Floor Mat, and on and on. What do you do with all this stuff? Organize it and store it where it's accessible to everyone who teaches kids at your church.

What are the options for storing all of these supplies? Your choices include a resource room, a closet, cabinets, or even storage at your house.

## Why do I need to organize my resources?
> - Enhance Bible-learning activities;
> - Be a good steward of the church's resources;
> - Support teachers by providing teaching resources; and
> - Cut down on waste and duplication of resources.

## How do I organize my resources?
- **Reserve a dedicated space.** This can be a cabinet, a closet, or a room. The space needs to be accessible to everyone who will use the resources.
- **Enlist a resource director.** Find a member of your church who is organized and enjoys shopping. Organizing and maintaining resources does take time, effort, and creativity, but can be fulfilling.
- **Organize your space.** You will need shelves for stacking boxes, baskets, buckets, picture files, and games. Pizza boxes will hold many types of items and can be stacked easily.
- **Allow leaders to request items.** Create an easy method for leaders to communicate their needs. A request form turned in with attendance sheets or a dry erase board in the resource room are effective ways to communicate.
- **Make a list of the items you want to have available.** Look ahead in the curriculum materials and see will be needed for the next quarter.
- **Involve the church in collecting resources.** Advertise for needed items so others can be involved in your ministry.

- **Plan your space.** Decide on the types of shelving and containers you are going to use, depending on where your resources will be stored.
- **Sort items for easy access.** Sort items by activity: art, blocks, homeliving, music, puzzles and manipulatives, and nature. Sorting items by subject is also an easy way for leaders to find additional resources for teaching (Jesus, God, church, self, and so forth).
- **Make items easy to find.** Label all shelves and bins and make a master list. Using a computer spreadsheet software program can help you organize your list. Items may be sorted in alphabetical order or by bin number. Place a copy of this list in each classroom so the leaders can see if a needed item is in the resource room.
- **Search your rooms for items that are not used every week.** Storing these items in a place other than classrooms helps the children stay focused on the current lesson.
- **Do not be afraid to throw some things away.** Kids leaders are notorious for saving everything they might need someday. If an item has not been used in a year or two, throw it away.
- **Share space with other ministries.** The music ministry could store music supplies. The recreation ministry could store outdoor play items. Make a list of those items available for everyone to share.

## How do I know what to keep and what to throw away?

Remember the three *Rs* of keeping resources:

- **Reuse**—Is this resource reusable? After the resource has been used, will you be able to find another use for it? If the answer is yes, then keep it. Reusable items include gameboards, game pieces, specialty paints, and markers.
- **Recycle**—In other words, throw it away. If the items are damaged or used up, "Throw them away." If toys or games have broken parts, "Throw them away."
- **Re-shelve**—Once items are used in a room, encourage leaders to return items to their proper storage places.

*Cindy Lumpkin and Carla Vied*

.......... ................................................................................................

*For more information on organizing your resources,*
*check out the following items on the Kids Ministry 101 CD-ROM:*
"Basic Resources for Kids Ministry," Item24
"Resource Rescue," Item 25

# Chapter 16

# What About Leadership Meetings and Training?

## Why are leadership meetings important?

The leadership for some churches and kids ministries has removed the weekly leadership meetings from their calendars due to busy people and busy churches. Some leaders even feel that those meetings are a waste of time. Others, however, view the meetings as a time to solve problems and plan the work of the ministry. Why are leadership meetings essential to effective ministry?

The purpose of leadership meetings is to provide a scheduled time for leaders to come together to focus on the mission of the church as it relates to the lives of children, to focus on the relationships among leaders and teachers, and to focus on Bible study that is critical in laying biblical foundations in the lives of children. Leadership meetings provide a scheduled time for teachers to pray together, asking God for spiritual guidance and direction for the ministry, and to organize the work of the ministry. Leadership meetings help teachers to be more effective in all aspects of kids ministry.

## When should I schedule meetings?

Schedule regular leadership meetings. However, if your church schedule does not allow weekly meetings, meet bi-weekly or monthly.

## How do I avoid leadership-meeting roadblocks?

- **Roadblock 1:** "My ministry is too small." Regardless of size, teachers need to be well prepared to provide a valuable experience for children. Use the meeting time to prepare for growth. Ask yourself the following questions: "Are the children who are attending worship service or special events enrolled in Sunday School?" or "Are we reaching children in the community?"
- **Roadblock 2:** "I don't have time." When teachers commit to serving girls and boys, help them understand that leadership meetings must

be a priority. What a great investment of time to reach and teach children! Meetings that are effectively conducted provide time for teachers to plan, gather resources, and understand biblical content.

## What are the benefits of leadership meetings?

- **Benefit 1:** Cultivating team spirit—Teachers and leaders develop a sense of unity and oneness. Lines of communication are open and clear for the team when teachers can contribute to the total work of the ministry.
- **Benefit 2:** Becoming well prepared—The meeting helps teachers gain a better understanding of the content of the Bible study. When teachers plan, they can bring all parts of the session together.
- **Benefit 3:** Receiving ongoing training—The meeting can offer teachers curriculum training as plans are made and discussed. Teachers can suggest ways to improve activities and make them better suited for the kids they teach.
- **Benefit 4:** Understanding childhood development—The meeting helps teachers to better understand the lives of kids and their families. Knowing information about how kids learn and grow can help teachers meet individual needs.

## How do I keep teachers coming back to meetings?

- **Make a commitment.** Teachers must understand their commitment to building biblical foundations in the lives of children. When teachers commit to the ministry team, a ministry description list should include, as one of the responsibilities, attending regularly scheduled meetings. Knowing their commitment will bring teachers back!
- **Send meeting reminders.** Send an e-mail notice or, when possible, give a call reminding teachers of the meeting. A friendly reminder will bring them back!
- **Develop an agenda.** Design an agenda that includes teacher involvement in the meeting. Teachers can lead Bible study, report on special activities, provide brief training, and review articles from preschool and children's magazines. Being a participant will bring them back!
- **Always start on time.** Arrive early to have the room ready and materials available. Respect those who show up on time by beginning promptly with prayer. Using time wisely will bring them back!
- **Use a variety of methods for leading the meeting.** Teaching methods used with preschoolers and children can be incorporated into your meetings. For example, use role play or games to tell the

Bible story. Use scenarios to discuss techniques to manage the classroom environment or handle children's behavior in positive ways. For fun, play a cell phone game to see how many kids the teachers can contact in fifteen minutes. Variety will bring them back!

- **Use multi-media materials.** View and discuss DVDs such as *Leading a Child to Christ* or *Worship Kid Style* designed specifically for kids. Using more of their senses will bring them back!
- **Show teacher appreciation and support.** Encourage teachers and find a variety of ways to let them know that you care. Provide home-baked goodies and small gifts to show them you appreciate their efforts. Caring for others will bring them back!
- **Allow time for open discussion.** Give teachers opportunities to share their teaching successes and funny moments with children. Laughter will bring them back!
- **End on time.** End meetings on time, reflecting on the positive. Pray for the children and their families, and pray for one another, thanking God for the opportunity to serve. Prayer will bring them back!
- **Evaluate the leadership meetings.** Gather feedback on ways to improve the meetings. Ask for suggestions of topics for other meetings. Letting leaders have their say will bring them back!
- **Keep track of attendance.** Finding out why teachers are not attending communicates a caring attitude. Absent teachers may be in school, attending sporting events with their children, traveling for business, or experiencing a personal problem or illness. Accountability for attendance and concern for others will bring them back!

### What are the steps for planning leadership meetings?

The content of the leadership meeting is divided into three parts focusing on mission, relationship, and Bible study.

- **Mission**—This part of the leadership meeting addresses churchwide events in conjunction with the childhood ministry. For example, if the church is planning discipleship training for adults, what plans are made for the kids? Evaluate events planned specifically for children, such as an ice cream party or a back-to-school fellowship. Address ministry concerns like classroom space and curriculum needs.
- **Relationship**—During this portion of the leadership meeting, give emphasis to reaching kids and developing relationships with them and their families. Invite teachers to give reports on their contacts and visits. Plan ways to respond to the needs of kids and their families. Plan fellowship activities, like a skating party or open house, and discuss them with the ministry team.

- **Bible study**—Devote part of the leadership meeting to Bible study. Help teachers plan together, and seek the most appropriate ways for teaching biblical truths. Teachers can review the Bible story and the Bible-learning activities, share ideas, and look at supplementary activities that can enhance the Bible-centered activities.

The leadership meeting provides unity to help teachers and leaders to be their best so that they can do their best for kids. Well-planned leadership meetings can help teachers make lasting impressions on children.

## Why is it important that I train my leaders?

Trained and prepared kids leaders are essential to building a strong kids ministry. The difference between an average learning experience for a child and a great one is dependent on worker preparation. "Lord, bless us according to our preparation" is a prayer few are willing to pray. Why not make a difference in your ministry and begin your preparation with a workers training event?

## What are some ways I can train my leaders?

- **State/associational training**—States and associations offer excellent training opportunities, usually at no cost. Conferences are available for specific training for the different aspects of your kids ministry such as Sunday School, discipleship training, missions, music, recreation, and Vacation Bible School. You name it, and many of our state and associational training teams will cover it. Check with your state convention or association to see when training events will be held.
- **Individual church training events**—Sometimes, because of scheduling conflicts, you just can't get your workers to the state or associational training events. If that's the case, then schedule a training event for your workers at your church. Find a date on the church calendar, and plan an event that will not only serve as a training time, but a kickoff for the excitement of a new church year or a special event. An added bonus to having individual training events is that your group can deal with specific issues that relate only to your church (schedules, needs, procedures, and so forth).
- **Sunday after church**—Schedule your event to follow morning worship/Sunday School. Provide a quick lunch for your workers followed by a time of training and preparation. Use a theme to launch your creative thinking in regards to the meal and the decorations. Give door prizes that teachers can use in decorating their rooms. After the meal, take a few minutes to share with your leaders specifics about

your ministry. Then move into groups for specific training (preschool, children, music, missions, and so forth).

- **Multiply opportunities**—We will never get everyone's schedule to coordinate, so why not offer training more than once. Give your workers the option of two training dates. The two dates might be your association event and the event you plan at your church. Or consider teaming up with another church in the community for a joint training event. Sometimes other churches in your area are using the same curriculum. Invite them to team with your church to provide multiple training opportunities.
- **Mini training events**—Think about the possibility of having a series of fifteen-minute training times at your regular planning meetings. For example, you could train preschool leaders on hygiene policies and train children's leaders on how to use games to teach Bible skills.
- **Round robin training**—Divide the training sessions into multiple subjects. Take four different subjects, enlist four of your best teachers to prepare one subject each, and rotate your workers through all four sessions. This helps your trainers not to be so overwhelmed by the preparation of training. It also helps your teachers see more than just one approach to teaching. Preschool leaders might need conferences on homeliving, puzzles, art, and nature. Children's leaders might need conferences on using drama, research, games, and telling a Bible story.
- **Sunday during Sunday School**—Consider conducting training during the actual Sunday School time. Enlist parents to substitute for teachers while they train. Record attendance is guaranteed!

## What topics should I use for training my leaders?
- **For preschool teachers**
  - ➤ how to use learning centers
  - ➤ how to teach babies and ones
  - ➤ safety and hygiene
  - ➤ how to reach families through phone calls, cards, e-mails, and visits
  - ➤ ideas for art, homeliving, nature, blocks, puzzles, and games
  - ➤ how to make group time exciting and fun
- **For children's teachers**
  - ➤ children and salvation
  - ➤ how children learn
  - ➤ differences in learning styles of boys and girls
  - ➤ how to use music, art, research, drama, and small group activities
  - ➤ how to make the most of group time
  - ➤ how teaching boys is different from teaching girls

- how children worship God
- how to develop children's Bible skills
- **For both preschool and children**
  - how to use the curriculum
  - *Levels of Biblical Learning™*
  - Levels of Bible Skills
  - how children develop spiritually
  - how to reach families
  - how to plan for Sunday morning
- **For your ministry leadership team**
  - how to work as a team
  - how to build a budget
  - how to lead planning meetings
  - how to enlist teachers

## How do I plan a leadership training event?

- **Making advance preparations**
  - Look at your church calendar and set a date for the training event.
  - Enlist a team of volunteers to help you with planning and preparation.
  - Decide on a theme for the event.
  - Promote the event by e-mailing or mailing invitations to each leader. Encourage attendance and state when and where the event is being held.
  - Provide a three-ring binder for each volunteer. Include information pertinent to your church and to teaching preschoolers and children. Some ideas include the following:
    1. Department roll: names of children or children and leaders complete with addresses, phone numbers, birth dates, parents' names, and so forth.
    2. Instructions on how your church completes attendance, outreach, and visitation records.
    3. *Levels of Biblical Learning™* and Levels of Bible Skills (available from Lifeway Christian Resources).
    4. A written job description, or a list of requirements and expectations for leaders at your church.
    5. A copy of your church's policies related to security and other relevant issues.
- **Preparing the training environment**
  - Arrange the room with enough adult-size tables and chairs to accommodate your group.

- Make a fun centerpiece that fits your chosen theme. Avoid themes related to guns or weapons.
- Place a ministry binder in each chair.
- Make your leaders feel appreciated by providing refreshments and a gift of appreciation like a pencil with your kids ministry logo or an inspirational bookmark.

- **Building morale**

Many times, preschool and children's leaders feel more like glorified baby-sitters rather than a vital part of your church.

- Invite your pastor to start your training event with words of affirmation and encouragement to build morale.
- Enlist experienced leaders to share stories about blessings they have received from teaching preschoolers and children.
- Ask new leaders to share why they have chosen to teach preschoolers or children.

Explain that everyone must work together to achieve a common goal. Help your leaders understand that they may work with different age groups, but all of them have the same mission. That mission is to reach kids and their families with the love of God and to help them grow in a personal relationship with Jesus.

- **Understanding the goal**

There is a saying, "If you aim at nothing you will hit it every time." So what is your goal? Use age-specific resources to help your leaders understand developmental characteristics of the age they teach. Also, *Levels of Biblical Learning* is an easy-to-follow chart that breaks down the spiritual development of children. Order resources online at *www.lifeway.com/kids*.

- **Overcoming obstacles to effective teaching**

- In order for a leader to be effective, he must understand his assignment, work alongside his team, and stay focused on the mission. These same principles apply to leaders. Help your leaders understand their assignments by reviewing the basic requirements for leaders at your church.
- Explain how to use your Sunday School curriculum and share information about additional resources or Web sites available.
- Make sure leaders understand that teaching preschoolers and children does not just happen on Sunday mornings. But weekly preparation, outreach, and ministry are also part of their Sunday School commitment.

- ➤ Encourage each class to work together as a team. Sometimes one person may try to do all the work of the class by herself. Explain to your leaders how critical it is to share responsibilities.
- **Ending with a covenant**
  - ➤ Create volunteer covenant cards that read: "Considering the great things the Lord has done for me, I will serve Him faithfully with all my heart in teaching children."
  - ➤ Invite each leader to sign a card and place it in his/her Bible as a reminder of the commitment to the Lord and to preschoolers and children.
  - ➤ Close in prayer, recognizing that God is the ultimate leader of your kids ministry and entrusting each boy, girl, parent, and volunteer to Him.

Why are planning and training important to the success of your kids ministry? In a recent study, parents were asked what they wanted from their kids leaders. Overwhelmingly, they responded trained, prepared teachers. In kids ministry, qualified adults to teach is a mandate and the key to a successful ministry.

*Mary DePass, Bill Emeott, and Cindy Lumpkin*

*For more information on leadership training for your kids ministry, check out the following items on the Kids Ministry 101 CD-ROM:*
*"Planning Leadership Meetings," Item 26*
*"10 Quick Training Tips," Item 27*
*"3 Kids Ministry Training Events," Item 28*

# Chapter 17

# How Do I Build Ministry Networks?

*A friend loves at all times. Proverbs 17:17a*

Ministry is a lot like fishing. Fishing can be lots of fun, but when done alone with one pole, it's time consuming, lonely, and generally does not net many fish. Fishing is hard work. Given the opportunity to fish with a net and a group of fishermen can be more efficient, effective, and fun. Developing a large ministry network brings the same results as fishing with a net.

## Why build a network?

- You don't need to make all the mistakes.
- You don't know everything.
- You are not gifted in all areas required to do ministry.
- You can help others.
- You need friends who will listen and encourage you.
- You need someone who will tell you the truth, even when it's hard to hear.
- You can discover prospects and opportunities for ministry.

Developing a large network to meet your expanding ministry needs brings amazing results. Build a network within the church with staff and volunteers to support your ministry. Build a network with peers in ministry for insights. Build a network in the community for outreach and ministry to others. Your networks should include but not be limited to people …

- in similar situations.
- in very different situations.
- like you and different from you.
- with varying levels of experience.
- with gifts and talents different from yours.
- involved in targeted groups for outreach and ministry.

Developing relationships with others in ministry and in the community multiplies your skills. Talking with someone outside of the situation often provides a different perspective. Others may come up with the perfect solution that you can't believe you didn't think of yourself. Through networking relationships you can gain valuable information.

- ➤ Do others face similar challenges?
- ➤ What has worked?
- ➤ What has not worked?
- ➤ How do they implement ministry plans?
- ➤ What would they do differently given the opportunity?
- ➤ What opportunities are there for ministry and outreach?

Often times you may think you do not have time to network. You let your to-do list rule your life. Networking is like taking a deep breath when you're exercising and wanting to give up. It is oxygen for ministry lungs. Make networking a priority.

Networks can be emotional support systems that keep you in ministry. The encouragement and support can be invaluable. Much like tired and discouraged fishermen, networks come alongside you and help to hold the net. Over the years I have observed that children's ministers with the longest tenure also tend to have the largest network—not just because they have been in ministry for years but also because they have understood the value of encouragement and advice from others.

## What are ways to network?

- ➤ joining Internet networking groups
- ➤ attending conferences and seminars
- ➤ forming a group of kids leaders that meets regularly.
- ➤ purposely visiting other churches
- ➤ visiting community groups and organizations to see how your ministry might benefit them
- ➤ actively serving/joining a service group in the community

Your networking must be intentional. It does not just happen. You must make it happen. Just like fishermen, if you don't put the net in the water, you won't catch any fish. Not only must networking be intentional, but it also must be continuous. Networking is never finished but must be continually nourished and expanded.

*Clara Mae VanBrink*

# Instruction?

## You mean I need more than a Bible?

**R**achel, John, and Brady sat around the art table, painting. "I need the blue paint," said John.

"I'll trade," said Rachel.

As the kindergartners painted and traded colors, I asked them about what they were doing. We talked about the Bible story. The children talked about Jesus and about what they were painting.

"In a verse in the Bible Jesus said, 'Love one another,'" I said. "That's what you're doing." The children continued to paint and didn't comment.

"Oh, well," I thought. "At least I tried."

Later in group time, I read the Bible verse again, "Jesus said, 'Love one another.'"

Rachel spoke up, "That's what we were doing."

Startled, I asked, "What?"

"When we were painting," she explained. "We were trading paint. We were loving one another."

*R. Scott Wiley*

And that from childhood you have known the sacred Scriptures, which are able to instruct you for salvation through faith in Christ Jesus.
**2 Timothy 3:15**

# Chapter 18
# How Do I Choose Curriculum?

*All Scripture is inspired by God and is profitable for teaching, for rebuking, for correcting, for training in righteousness. 2 Timothy 3:16*

Choosing Bible study curriculum for girls and boys is one of the most important decisions your church will make. The quality of the curriculum will directly influence the spiritual growth of each child in your church. As you think about choosing curriculum, make sure your choice provides the following qualities:

- **Activity Anchored:** A variety of activities helps kids do more than hear God's Word: they experience it. One-year-olds through kindergartners learn at their own pace by choosing to participate in Bible-learning centers such as art, blocks, nature, homeliving, and puzzles. First through sixth graders engage in learning through crafts, drama, writing, music, and games.
- **Bible Based:** The Bible is the center of the curriculum. If an activity does not relate to the Bible passage, then it doesn't need to be part of the session. Ask yourself: "Does the curriculum have a balanced scope and sequence? Are the Bible stories true to the biblical text? Is the life application based on Bible truth?"
- **Child Centered:** Bible-learning activities are designed with the child in mind. Age-appropriate activities are suitable to the age group and relate to the interests and abilities of each child. *Levels of Biblical Learning*™ defines what biblical concepts kids need to learn and at what ages they need to learn them.
- **Doctrinally Dependable:** The curriculum must be based on sound, biblical doctrine. The materials need to lay foundations for kids to understand basic biblical truths.
- **Educationally Sound:** Curriculum should be designed to engage kids on their level of understanding and to teach them in the ways they learn best. Large- and small-group activities need to relate to all learning styles and approaches.
- **Foundationally Firm:** Bible truths, Bible stories, and Bible verses help kids build foundations of basic truths that will guide them throughout their lives. These truths are about God, Jesus, Bible, Creation, Family, Self, Church, Community and World, Holy Spirit, and Salvation.

- **Good Choices:** Giving kids choices is a basic principle in teaching preschoolers and children. Kids can make choices about Bible-learning centers, activities, and ways to express what they've learned.
- **Hands-on Experiences:** Curriculum should invite kids to participate in hands-on experiences. Kids of all ages need to be actively involved in the learning process.
- **Imitation Intended:** Your goal is to be Christlike. Your example to them should allow kids to grasp truth from your lifestyle and their relationship with you as you teach them with words and activities. As kids grow older, they will not recall every Bible lesson, but they will remember you.
- **Jesus:** The reason for Bible study is to introduce kids to Jesus. With babies, the journey toward Jesus begins as they learn that He loves them and continues as older kids learn that Jesus' crucifixion, burial, and resurrection were a necessary part of God's plan for the forgiveness of sin.
- **Knowledge Gained:** One of the goals of teaching kids at church is to help them gain Bible knowledge. Kids need to learn the Bible stories and Bible verses that will guide them through life. In addition to biblical knowledge, kids need to learn how to apply biblical truth to their lives.
- **Leader Accountability:** Accountability means being committed, following through with responsibilities, and caring for kids. Ministry leaders and volunteers are accountable to God, their churches, their peers, and the children they teach. Planning times, teaching times, and fellowship times are all expressions of commitment.
- **Ministry Minded:** Curriculum should include ideas for reaching and ministering to kids and their families. Curriculum can also encourage workers to involve kids in age-suitable ministry.
- **Needs Met:** Kids today have a variety of needs. Curriculum can't meet all those needs, but you and your children's leaders and workers can provide kids with love, acceptance, security, and guidance.
- **Outlandish:** Kids want to have fun. Curriculum needs to include opportunities for kids to laugh and enjoy their times at church.
- **Preparation:** The best Bible study sessions require teacher preparation. When a teacher invests time in his own Bible study and session preparation, he can engage kids in meaningful Bible study experiences.
- **Quality Expected:** Curriculum materials should be biblically sound with age-suitable activities that help kids hear, know, and do God's Word. Look for materials that are written, edited, and designed well.

- **Real Relationships:** Real relationships take time. When workers make a commitment to teach kids, they are making a time commitment. They're also making a commitment to a relationship with the kids in their classrooms—taking time to get to know them, to know how they learn best, to know how to communicate with them, and to know where each child stands in his or her relationship with Jesus.
- **Steps Toward Conversion:** Curriculum should help kids on their journey toward becoming Christians. Bible study, stories, activities, and discussions can guide kids to the point where they can respond when the Holy Spirit moves in their hearts.
- **Transformational:** Spiritual transformation is the goal of Bible study for babies through preteens. It begins with teachers and their personal Bible study, and then moves to the sessions where kids encounter Bible truths and apply them to their everyday lives.
- **Units of Study:** Units of study allow teachers and children to focus on one biblical concept area for four to six sessions, using a variety of teaching methods. As kids study Joseph, Ruth, or David for a month, they can explore many facets of the lives of those people and make application to their own lives. As kids study units on the Bible, they can discover how the Bible came to be and how God used people to protect and preserve the Bible.
- **Video-Enhanced:** Curriculum can capture kids' attention with a short video clip while retaining kids' relationships with teachers. This method is preferable to video-driven curriculum that lessens opportunities for teachers to build strong relationships with kids.
- **Worldview:** As kids lay foundations for spiritual growth, they are also laying foundations for a biblical worldview. How a child sees God, herself, and the world is directly related to Bible teaching and her practice of what she learns.
- **Xcellent Resources:** You want to expect excellence in curriculum materials. Look for quality, good design, outstanding art, fun music, well-written sessions, and the way all the curriculum pieces fit together. A curriculum evaluation tool can help you compare the materials from different publishers and then make the best choice for your church and your kids.
- **Your Family:** A curriculum for kids must also help parents assume their responsibilities as the primary biblical teachers of their children. Curriculum can encourage parents to, "Repeat them [God's teachings] to your children. Talk about them when you sit in your house and when you walk along the road, when you lie down and when you get up" (Deuteronomy 6:7).

- **Zip, Zest, Zoom:** Some curriculum materials make promises about zip, zest, and zoom—curriculum that will almost teach itself. All you need to do is open the lid. Beware! Sometimes you may find curriculum at a low cost and think, "Wow, what a bargain!" Remember, you get what you pay for. If quality Bible study materials are what your church needs, then take time to investigate and purchase curriculum that will meet the needs of your kids. Let the zip, zest, and zoom come in the teachers' excitement over the Bible study, in the response of the kids to the activities and experiences, and in the parents' approval of the biblical training their children are receiving.

*Landry R. Holmes and Judy H. Latham*

*For more information on the Levels of Biblical Learning, Levels of Bible Skills, and evaluating curriculum, check out the following items on the Kids Ministry 101 CD-ROM:*
"Levels of Biblical Learning," Item 2
"Levels of Bible Skills," Item 3
"Evaluating Curriculum," Item 29

# Chapter 19
# How Do I Make the Most of Sunday Morning?

*Listen, Israel: The LORD our God, the LORD is One. Love the LORD your God with all your heart, with all your soul, and with all your strength. These words that I am giving you today are to be in your heart. Repeat them to your children. Talk about them when you sit in your house and when you walk along the road, when you lie down and when you get up. Deuteronomy 6:4-7*

## Why Sunday School?

Sunday School will be the largest, continuously attended event in the life of your church. Vacation Bible School may have more participants, but Sunday School is an ongoing ministry that consistently touches the lives of many more children. Consider the following reasons for the importance of Sunday morning:

> As it is continuously running, Sunday School will serve as the largest evangelistic tool your church will use to help boys and girls come to know Jesus Christ as personal Lord and Savior.

> Sunday School provides a designated time for studying the Bible and learning foundational spiritual truths.

> Sunday School provides teachers opportunities each week to minister to boys and girls through one-on-one experiences.

> Sunday School gives kids the opportunity to minister to one another through peer relationships. Peer interactions may one day lead a child to come to know Jesus Christ as personal Lord and Savior.

> Sunday School should be the main focus of your ministry experiences each week. Not to say that other organizations are not important, but Sunday School should be the focus of your Sunday morning time together.

> Your church may choose to use a different term than Sunday School. However, whatever name you use, your church should provide a weekly Bible study experience for boys and girls.

## How should I organize my Sunday School?

Create classes of children grouped by age. The number of classes and the age range of each class will depend on the number of children attending Sunday School. Within each class, teachers should provide large-group experiences and small-group experiences.

## Why use large-group experiences?

> ➤ Large-group times (when all the kids are together) help children hear God's Word, know God's Word, and do God's Word.
> ➤ Large-group experiences help to pull all of the learning together.
> ➤ Large-group experiences are primarily teacher directed. A teacher will facilitate this part of the class to deliver appropriate content and information.
> ➤ Large-group experiences may help leaders to maintain control of children while learning is going on.
> ➤ Large-group experiences give opportunities for focused learning on a key Bible truth, an age-appropriate life application, and an introduction of key Bible verses.
> ➤ Large-group times are designed to help teachers deliver information in a planned and systematic way to guide girls and boys on an adventure of Bible discovery.
> ➤ Large-group times can give kids an opportunity to open God's Word and begin to learn how to use the Bible to guide them as they continue to grow.

## Why use small-group experiences?

> ➤ Small-group experiences (when kids are together in multiple small groups) help children hear God's Word, know God's Word, and do God's Word. Kids learn to use the Bible and apply what they learn.
> ➤ Small-group experiences facilitate more peer-to-peer interactions among the kids.
> ➤ Small-group experiences give kids better opportunity to discover Bible truths through self-discovery.
> ➤ Small-group experiences provide a greater opportunity for hands-on learning.
> ➤ Small-group learning enables kids to apply the Bible truth and to make specific application to their daily lives.
> ➤ Small-group learning is typically more child directed than leader directed. Kids may work at their own pace to facilitate learning.
> ➤ Large groups and small groups will both have importance in a Sunday morning experience.

**How do I, as a ministry professional, make the most of the Sunday morning experience?**

- **Pray!** Pray specifically for leaders in your ministry.
- **Decide that Sunday School is important for kids.**
- **Develop policies and procedures to guide parents and children to enjoy their time at church on Sunday morning.**
- **Organize your Sunday School departments to best meet the needs of your church.** Consider appropriate needs for furniture, time frame, number of classrooms, curriculum, supplies, and other teaching resources.
- **Ask God to lead you to the right people to fill key ministry positions.** God wants your ministry to succeed as much as you do. Find the right, God called, people to serve as teachers, directors, and in other leadership positions.
- **Provide necessary and adequate training to help the leaders whom God has given you to become the best at teaching His truths.**
- **Be prepared with a list of trained volunteers to fill any unexpected teacher or key leader absences.** Sometimes things happen on Sunday morning outside of your control. If this happens, be prepared to solve the problem with relative ease.
- **Support and encourage teachers and other leaders in your ministry group.** Provide opportunities for leadership to feel valued as the called-by-God leaders they are. Consistently and genuinely encourage the people who serve in the kids ministry.
- **Maintain a consistent and reliable form of security for your church's preschool and children's ministries.** Ensuring the safety of boys and girls will help facilitate a smooth transition from home to Sunday School and from Sunday School to worship.
- **As leaders arrive, engage in one-on-one conversations** to determine what needs have yet to be met before kids begin to arrive. Be sure to meet those specific needs in a timely manner.
- **As children begin to arrive, identify and greet new visitors.** Ensure that visitors and their parents are escorted personally to the appropriate classrooms. Parents will need to know where their child's classroom is located when they return.
- **Engage boys and girls in one-on-one conversations in the hallways before they arrive at their classrooms.** Building relationships with kids will help them know that church is a place they can come to feel welcomed and accepted.

## How do I, as a Sunday School teacher, make the most of the Sunday morning experience?

- **Pray!** Pray by name for each child on your roll.
- **Greet each child by name as he enters the door.** Direct the child immediately to an activity you prepared for the beginning of class.
- **Maintain records of attendance and record any prayer needs the girls and boys mention.**
- **If children arrive prior to the start of Sunday School,** engage in one-on-one conversations to help build relationships with each child in your classroom.
- **Establish appropriate class rules.** Involve kids in developing a short list of rules. Guide the boys and girls to follow the rules to help facilitate learning.
- **Come prepared to teach the lesson for Sunday.** Use teachable moments provided by the Holy Spirit to guide discovery learning.
- **Provide opportunities for boys and girls to learn through both large-group and small-group experiences.**
- **Give kids appropriate tools to discover biblical truths and make applications to their own lives.**

*Tim Pollard and R. Scott Wiley*

# Chapter 20
# How Do I Teach in a Non-Traditional Setting?

*Then they spoke the message of the Lord to him along with everyone in his house. Acts 16:32*

Many churches no longer meet in traditional church facilities. They hold services in non-traditional places such as schools, movie theaters, warehouses, and storefronts. Most of these churches are referred to as "set up and tear down churches." They are faced with challenges uncommon to the traditional church. As more and more of these congregations begin to meet in these places, sharing knowledge of how others have established children's ministries in these non-traditional environments is imperative.

### What are basic steps to take in building a non-traditional ministry?

- Establish policies, procedures, and security guidelines.
- Recruit and train volunteers in the following three areas: 1) set up and tear down team, 2) welcome center and greeting team, and 3) teachers. Remember, this ministry cannot happen without the help of volunteers. So show them appreciation in as many ways as you can throughout the year.
- Utilize your church's Web site and Web-based social networks to communicate with families. Provide ideas for ways parents can continue to teach biblical truths kids learn at church and at home.
- Plan mid-week opportunities to connect with your church families. Some simple and great ways to do this are through play dates, lunch groups, and book clubs. These opportunities allow church members to get to know each other and also provide a great way to reach out to unchurched families in your community.
- Create awareness of the church's kids ministry by hosting community-wide events such as block parties, parents' night out, pool parties, skate nights, and other fun, family activities.

One challenge you will face each week is preparing the learning environment for your kids ministry. This requires much logistical planning and preparation. The tasks required can be divided into two main areas.

## How do I set up a learning environment?

- Use dividers and gates to divide large spaces into smaller "classroom" areas.
- Use carpets and mats to create soft floor space.
- Take pictures of the classroom after it is set up to provide volunteers with a visual for how the room should look. Display the picture with a list of all setup steps in a checklist format to help volunteers remember all that needs to be done. An example is included on the *Kids Ministry 101 CD-ROM*.
- Enlist committed volunteers to help with setup and teardown. Being able to rely on the same group of people to assist each week will ensure that the learning environment itself is consistent from week to week.
- Transport tables, lights, storage bins, and other supplies on rolling carts or in rolling cribs.
- Clean tables, mats, and toys before and after each session with disinfecting wipes. Provide a vacuum to clean carpets each week.
- Hang signs at the entrance of each room giving the age of the children and the names of the teachers.
- Secure all entries and exits to the children's area.
- Create a welcome center at the entrance of the children's area. Distribute security tags, allergy alert tags, visitor cards, and ministry information at this table.

## How do I store my supplies during the week?

- Organize classroom supplies into storage bins. Label each bin, carpet, light, table, and other items that go into each room with an identifying number.
- Use clear storage bins so you can see the contents of each bin. These tend to get messy if not monitored closely. Extra items can quickly find their way into the bins, and you certainly don't want any extra weight when loading and unloading every week!
- Store like items in the same bin, and try to limit the number of bins per classroom to a maximum of four bins. For example, set aside one bin for diaper changing supplies, cleaning supplies, snack cups, napkins, and hand sanitizer. In a second bin, store curriculum, teacher supplies, and art supplies. In the last two bins store toys, manipulatives, blocks, and other teaching materials.
- Ask your location for some on-site storage, if possible. Use this space to store tables, chairs, and larger supplies that are difficult to carry and load and unload on a truck.

- If you are not provided enough on-site storage, acquire a truck or trailer for storage of supplies.
- Use cribs with locking wheels or portable cribs for the infant and toddler rooms. Rolling cribs are also great for transporting the supply bins and other equipment.

## What do I need to provide for children during small-group Bible studies at members' homes?

- Find a location that will allow you to have mid-week Bible study activities. Secure the location on a weekly basis. Parents can choose to be a part of a small-group meeting at the same time.
- Child care for preschoolers can be held in one part of a home while Bible study for adults meets in another part. If two church members live close together, child care can be provided in one house while the Bible study group meets in the other house.
- Decide on who will take care of the kids at each location. Consider asking adults from another small group to lead the preschoolers and children.
- Since many families attend church only one hour on Sunday in a non-traditional setting, the weekly Extended Teaching Care resources can be used during child care to reinforce biblical truths.
- Another great resource to use for planning mid-week activities for childcare is LifeWay's EXTRA! (To see an example of EXTRA! go to *www/lifeway.com/extra.*)
- Groups will usually have a variety of ages in one room, so plan accordingly with a variety of age-level activities.

While children's ministry in a non-traditional setting can be challenging, it can also be fun and rewarding. This type of ministry has the potential to reach many families that would not attend a more traditional church. Knowing that you are helping families experience Christ and grow in a relationship with Him makes all the hard work worthwhile.

*Danette Cravens*

*For more information on setting up Bible teaching space in a non-traditional setting, check out the following item on the Kids Ministry 101 CD-ROM:*
"Setting Up Bible-teaching Experiences in a Non-Traditional Space," Item 30

# Chapter 21
# How Do I Minister to Kids with Special Needs?

*I will praise You, because I have been remarkably and wonderfully made. Your works are wonderful, and I know this very well. Psalm 139:14*

The most critical ministry decision a leader will encounter is one that has no clear-cut answer and requires immediate action. In most cases, this is what you will face when a family with a child with special needs unexpectedly arrives. With no advance warning, a family may enter just as classes are beginning. Your initial reaction and how you proceed may be the deciding factors in whether this family will return to your church.

## Why is your first reaction so important?

The reason can be found in how good ministry is perceived. As a leader, you are conditioned to prepare in advance for kids to come and participate in age-graded groupings. Your ministry has structure, routines, and the flow of parents and children who move smoothly to their designated classes. Good ministry meets the needs of the masses. However, for the family of a child with special needs, life is not about structure or routines, and it's certainly not smooth. The parents need additional time to communicate the needs of their child. For parents a good ministry is flexible, adaptable, and understanding.

## What are misconceptions about families with special needs that prevent you from reaching out and ministering to them?

- **Families expect the church to have the perfect plan in place for them.** Instead, families with a special needs child want a loving church family that will grow to love them and is sensitive to their needs.
- **A child with special needs has two options:** to participate in a self-contained class or to be main-streamed into a regular class. Because "special needs ministry" covers such a broad area, multiple options need to be available with the child's needs at the core.

So, next Sunday if a family with a special needs child walks through the door, do not panic. Give your full and undivided attention to this family. If there are siblings, lead the whole family to the appropriate class or classes. This is a wonderful time to show them the layout of the church and to introduce them to other leaders in the kids ministry.

Then, go to a place that will allow you the time to talk with the family about their child. Don't hurry this process—it may be your only time to talk. A follow-up visit may never happen.

The unanswered question that remains is where to place the child with special needs. Most churches will quickly answer that mainstreaming is the correct answer. Others feel strongly that a new class should be created. And in some rare cases, families have been told that efforts will be made to help them find another church that can better meet their needs. The plain truth is there are no magic formulas, no specific guidelines, and no one-size-fits-all strategies that can guide you in this decision.

### How can I make the best decisions that will minister both to the family and to the child with special needs?

Consider the following guidelines:

➤ Creating a loving environment for a child with special needs will require open communication with parents. Some parents will insist on one educational strategy for their child without compromise. In cases such as this, every effort within reason should be made to honor the wishes of the parents.

➤ Flexibility and teamwork are two key components for successful ministry. Encourage your kids ministry to evaluate how things are done. Every person who is part of the ministry will be impacted and must be willing to be a part of reaching the family of a child with special needs. Small changes can make huge differences.

➤ Leaders with a "ministry mentality" will believe that children with special needs will continue to change as they grow older and will be committed to help them hear the message of Jesus Christ in very clear and understandable ways.

➤ Kids with special needs may have the ability to participate independently in some activities, need assistance in others, and may not be able to participate in some at all. The goal is to help kids participate in as many activities as possible using their own abilities.

➤ Pray for your church as God begins to show you His plan for reaching and ministering to families with a child with special needs who desperately need a supportive and loving church family.

### What are some concrete guidelines I need to know?

• **Mainstreaming children involves change in the class.** Adaptations and special considerations will need to be made in classrooms for kids with special needs to experience success. Also, leaders need to be equipped to teach in ways that will include all of the students. This educational strategy is most successful with high-functioning children.

- **A self-contained class is an educational strategy for learning at a slower pace with more repetition,** and it involves a higher ratio of leaders to children. This type of class is used when children are unable to handle the tempo, process the concepts, or stay engaged in a typical class. A self-contained class does not necessarily meet for the entire class period. Peer interaction, socialization, and integration of kids should be included as part of your overall ministry plan.

### How can my church discover potential prospects for special needs ministry?

- Locate schools in your area that specifically teach preschoolers and children with special needs.
- Host informational seminars on different types of special needs.
- Host a support group for parents of children with special needs.
- Advertise in a community newspaper or newsletter.
- Send a mailer to houses in the community.
- Include information in your church's newsletter.
- Spread the information by word of mouth.

### How do I teach a child with ADHD?

- Make sure every child knows you are glad she has come.
- Plan times for all children to interact with one other. This will help teach the child with ADHD how to interact and build relationships.
- Put away resources that could cause distraction or misbehavior.
- Use positive and affirming comments when the child is successful.
- Keep rewards tangible.
- Provide a place for a child to go in case of inappropriate behavior.
- Provide a consistent class schedule from week to week.
- Make sure you have the attention of the child before giving important directions. If needed, ask the child to repeat the directions back to you.
- Post simple rules that are easily understood.
- Keep transition times to a minimum.
- Evaluate discipline measures with other leaders and the child's parents. Be positive and sensitive to everyone involved.
- Become an organizer for the child. Plan lessons and activities with a plan for step-by-step instructions.
- Plan work that requires greater attention early in the schedule.

# How do I teach a child with autism?

- A calm, positive, communication-based approach is necessary.
- Use a picture system to communicate where you are going, whom you will see, and what you will do next.
- Provide structure, schedule, and predictability.
- Use a ball or a beanbag to help kids recall Bible verses.
- Encourage kids to interact with others by working as partners.
- Use visual cues such as pictures to help with the Bible story and other activities in the class.
- Encourage the child to use her whole body in learning.
- Be sensitive to the noise and activity level in the room. Many children with autism are extremely sensitive to loud noises.

# How do I adapt activities for the hearing impaired?

- Make sure you have the child's attention before giving instructions.
- Remain stationary and face students.
- Seat a child with a hearing impairment close to the front.
- Wait for the kids to quiet down before giving instructions.
- Do not over exaggerate or slow your speaking.
- Close any door or window that provides distractions.
- Include visual support and hands-on activities. Point to key pictures or reinforce with actions the major concepts.
- Use videos and PowerPoint® presentations.
- Allow adequate time for all students to see and hear before moving forward or changing a picture or slide.
- Divide activity instructions into smaller parts.
- Provide checkpoints to ensure a child's complete understanding.
- Use facial expressions and gestures to reinforce emotions.
- Provide assistance that encourages independence.

*Carlton S. McDaniel, Jr.*

*For more information on ministering to kids with special needs, check out the following item on the Kids Ministry 101 CD-ROM: "Meeting the Cultural Needs of Children," Item 31*

# Chapter 22
# How Do I Lead Kids in Worship Experiences?

*Come, let us worship and bow down; let us kneel before the LORD our Maker.*
*Psalm 95:6*

## Can children worship?

Yes, kids can worship, but they do not all worship in the same way. Church leaders, working with parents, must decide what type of worship experiences to provide for kids.

## What types of worship experiences are appropriate for children?

The following are three options for providing worship opportunities:
- **Children's Worship**—a worship experience for children designed on children's levels of understanding and structured to touch the hearts and minds of children
- **Intergenerational/Congregational Worship**—a multi-age worship experience in which individuals of all ages worship together
- **Combination Worship**—a mixture of intergenerational and children's worship. During the combination worship experience, kids attend a part of the congregational worship time and are dismissed to their own worship experience prior to the sermon.

## How do preschoolers and children learn to worship?

Preschoolers and children learn to worship …
- by observing individuals around them.
- by participating with individuals around them.
- by feeling welcome as a part of the worshiping family.
- through first-hand experiences designed for their style of learning.
- by hearing and applying Bible content to their lives.
- by singing songs they can understand and apply to their lives.

## Which type of worship is appropriate for children?

The decision about which type of worship is most appropriate will impact the kids, their families, and the church. Churches need to provide worship times that meet the needs of kids and help kids develop positive attitudes for worshiping God.

In deciding which type of worship to provide for kids, consider ...
- What is the best way of guiding the kids in your church to worship?
- Why does the church desire this type of ministry to kids?
- What are the advantages of this type of worship?
- What are the disadvantages of this type of worship?
- What kind of impact will this type of worship have on the spiritual development of kids?
- How will this type of worship impact families?
- What does this type of ministry say to the community about the value of kids in your church?
- Is the purpose of this ministry for the good of the kids, the families, and the whole church?

Remember, leading effective worship not only involves kids; it involves parents, staff members, volunteer teachers, and the congregation.

## What aspects of worship should be included?
Worship, whether congregational or children's, should include the following elements:
- **Praise**—both singing and spoken words
- **Offering**
- **Scripture**—reading and explaining the Bible on the kids' levels of learning
- **Life Application**—guidance for kids to know how the Bible truth applies to their lives
- **Prayer**—both by adults and the kids
- **Use of the Bible**—by both adults and kids
- **Age-appropriate type of commitment**—answer the question: "What am I going to do with the biblical content?"
- **Personal involvement**—Worship should not be a "spectator" activity. Worshipers, kids and adults, should be personally involved.

## How can kids be included in congregational worship?
- Allow kids to read Scripture.
- Invite a child to pray aloud.
- Invite family units to read Scripture or pray aloud.
- Encourage the kids to stand when the congregation stands.
- Utilize vocabulary kids understand.
- Share illustrations related to kids' lives (school, play, television shows, and so forth).
- Allow the children to assist with receiving the offering.

- Invite kids to serve as greeters and welcome people to the worship.
- Provide offering envelopes for kids.
- Utilize a variety of visuals.
- Balance the use of abstract concepts with concrete situations kids can understand.
- Provide kids' sermons from time to time.
- Provide kids' bulletins designed around the Scripture passage.
- Provide positive role models for the kids to observe.
- Help kids feel welcome and a part of the worshiping family.
- Keep the attention span of kids in mind when planning worship.
- Intentionally plan for kids to be a part of the worship time.

## What ages should be included in children's worship?

Leaders in your kids ministry should help the church leadership decide for what ages children's worship or Extended Teaching Care will be provided.

Grouping of ages will vary depending on the size of your church. If you have a small group of children, you may wish to combine several age groups together. As your church grows, consider grouping children closer in age.

- Birth–3s Extended Teaching Care—Provide individual classes for these ages as necessary.
- 4s–Kindergarten—Extended Teaching Care or Children's Worship
- 1st–3rd Grades—Children's Worship
- 4th–6th Grades—Children's Worship

## How can kids transition from children's worship to congregational worship?

Kids need assistance in moving from children's worship to congregational worship.

- **Provide training for parents before the time arrives for their children to attend congregational worship.**
- **Expose the kids to congregational worship gradually.** Several months before children are expected to attend congregational worship, encourage parents to begin taking their kids with them to congregational worship a few minutes each week.
- **Plan an "I'm Going to Big Church Day."**
  - Introduce the church staff and their roles.
  - Provide stickers with special messages for kids to wear on the first day in congregational worship.
  - Define vocabulary used in the worship service.

➤ Guide the kids to understand what will take place during a congregational worship service.

- **Acknowledge the kids the first day they are in the worship service:**
  ➤ Invite the kids to stand or join the pastor at the altar.
  ➤ Invite the parents to stand. Acknowledge the stress they may experience as they help their kids transition to worship.
  ➤ Pray for the children.
  ➤ Ask individuals sitting near the kids and parents to pray for the kids.
  ➤ Encourage the congregation to welcome the kids and to be patient as they adjust to attending congregational worship.

## What are other considerations in guiding kids to worship?

➤ Rely on the Holy Spirit. Listen to God as you plan and lead worship.
➤ Maintain high expectations of leaders. Leaders will live up to the expectations placed on them.
➤ Remember the levels of learning of the kids.
➤ Provide a variety of learning activities.
➤ Use the Bible and guide kids to use their Bibles.
➤ Involve the kids.
➤ Utilize simple vocabulary.
➤ Select appropriate Bible passages.
➤ Utilize a variety of teaching methods.
➤ Provide quality space.
➤ Realize children's worship is not baby-sitting. Resist a "Let's take care of the kids while parents attend worship" mentality.
➤ Realize children's worship is not a "let's play big church" time. Children's worship should be designed as worship on the kids' levels, not adult worship designed for children to "play church."

For leaders in kids ministry, one of the greatest joys is to watch the faces of kids who are truly involved in worship experiences. As the kids sing, pray, give, listen, and learn to apply Bible truths to their lives, they are learning to worship God. Remember, kids need positive worship experiences, whether your church decides to provide children's worship or to encourage the kids' involvement in congregational worship.

*Todd Capps*

# Chapter 23
# When and How Do I Use Technology in My Ministry?

*Technology is just a tool. It is the teacher who facilitates learning through relationships by motivating the kids to work together.*

We've been a part of the technology age for a while now. As with any change, we tend to drag our feet and cling to "tradition" or what might be better called our "comfort zone." The children we teach are experiencing the world in a whole new way. They no longer play games on a board, view pictures in a photo album, or listen to tunes from a record player. Incorporating technology into preparation and teaching is easier than you think and adds another dimension to the learning process for preschoolers and children.

## How can I use technology in planning and preparation?

If you are not using the Internet while planning and preparing for any lesson or children's event, you are missing out on great resources. Never has a plethora of information been so accessible in one place. We've always known that people have a lot to say, but now everyone has a place for it to be read, heard, or seen. What kind of things might you be able to find on the World Wide Web? The better question might be, "What can't you find?" Available with just a few clicks of the mouse are the following:

- clip art
- craft ideas
- new and old music
- games and activities
- video clips
- decorating ideas
- lesson plans
- articles and publications on any and every topic imaginable
- missions ideas
- and so much more

## How do I search for ideas on the Web?

Start with what you know, your trusty search engine. Typing in a few key words or phrases will bring up the most popular and often most useful sites on the Internet.

- Be specific with your wording. If you can't find what you're looking for, then use more general terms.
- Blogs are best for creative insight with crafts, decorating, and activities.
- If you are researching facts, be sure to use a reliable and credible source. Blogs have a lot to say, but they are not always credible.

## Can blogging help?

Sometimes the best ideas and advice come from people just like you. Blogging is becoming more and more popular among people of all backgrounds and expertise. Various types of blogs exist. You might find "do-it-yourself" type crafts and decorations. You can read about what one ministry is doing to teach their children about missions. The possibilities are endless. But remember that what works for one ministry doesn't always work for another. Keep in mind the characteristics and needs of your church, ministry, and children.

You may have great Sunday School curriculum but sometimes wish it offered a few alternative activities. Chances are, you can find them on the Internet. Almost every major publisher has a Web site, and many offer extra downloadable resources for free on their sites. Be sure to check sites regularly. One helpful thing about the Internet is that sites can be updated quickly and often.

## How and when should I use multi-media in the classroom?

Kids explore with curiosity using all of their senses. Bringing in an extra element of technology may be the key to helping children remember what they've learned. Consider using several types of media in the classroom:
- music that uses Scripture and memory verses
- video clip that illustrates a portion of the Bible story
- projection of a Bible map
- worship music videos that have words and/or motions

## How much technology should I use?

There is a fine line between incorporating media into your lesson and letting the media do the teaching. Consider the following when using media in kids ministry:
- **Stay Connected.** You could write letters and make calls all day, but the most efficient way to stay connected is the Internet.
- **Communicate with leaders via e-mail.** This helps everyone stay on the same page.

- **Keep parents updated and involved.** They are crucial to your kids ministry. With Sunday morning and Wednesday night activities, children's choir, Vacation Bible School, fall festivals, and other special events, your ministry has a lot going on during the year. Use e-mail and your church's Web site to convey information.
- **Use an online invitation site when announcing and inviting individuals to meetings,** training sessions, appreciation dinners, and all church events.
- **Send an occasional thank-you.** You can do this in an e-mail, or use free online greeting cards called e-cards.
- **Make a video and post it to the Web if you have a special announcement.** Once you have posted your video to a media-sharing site, you can place a link to the video in your e-mail.
- **Consider starting a group in an online community.** Here you can post announcements and leave messages. Because of safety and legal issues, do not to place photos of kids online.
- **Start your very own online community.** Research and find a site that allows you to customize an online venue to fit the needs of your community. This also gives you greater control of content posted and members who can join.

### Where can I find additional ideas for Bible study?

LifeWay weekly produces additional ideas for use with kids in Bible Study, known as EXTRA! You can find additional teaching ideas for preschoolers and grades 1 through 6. Go to *lifeway.com/myextra* to find these ideas.

### It's not about the newest and the best. It's about the kids.

Not every church has access to all the media mentioned. Each church is as unique as the people in it. Know your kids and what helps them learn about God's Word and how they can apply it to their lives. As Christians, it isn't about what we have, but about what we do with what we do have. Whatever God has blessed your ministry with, be sure you are doing your utmost to use it for furthering His kingdom. And what better place to start than with His precious children!

*Erin Drawdy*

# Kids?

## When did "wired kids" stop referring to kids hyped up on sugar?

**K**ids are a joy and delight to teach. One thing I try to remember, however, is never to be shocked by what they say. "Mr. Tim, you have a hole in your hair." That is by far my favorite quote from any child I've ever taught. In his innocent way, this child reminded me of the work God is doing in my physical body. He didn't mean any disrespect; he only stated what he saw as fact.

As my young friend grows, he will also see God's handiwork all around him and will be guided by teachers who love and care for him. Teachers who understand the way he grows physically, socially, mentally, and spiritually will guide him well along the path God has laid out for him.

*Tim Pollard*

Don't you see that children are GOD'S best gift? the fruit of the womb his generous legacy?
**Psalm 127:3 (The Message)**

# Chapter 24
# What Do I Need to Know About Kids Today?

*And Jesus increased in wisdom and stature, and in favor with God and with people.*
*Luke 2:52*

Cell phones, digital music, HDTV, razor scooters, and dolls with an edgy look—today's culture is different from the world many of us grew up in. Computers have replaced books, and video games have replaced imaginations. All these influences cause kids today to lose the experiences that made our childhoods seem idyllic. Despite these differences, kids' needs, characteristics, and ways of learning remain unchanged.

## What are some general characteristics of kids?

- **Kids are literal-minded.** Children tend to think in concrete terms rather than in symbolic ones. When talking with kids, choose concrete words and explain biblical truths.
- **Kids need to be active.** Muscle control for both large and small muscles is still developing. Periods of sitting need to be interspersed with periods of activity. Use the children's desire to move by playing games, using Bibles, and letting kids help with different activities.
- **Kids need to succeed.** Planning age-appropriate activities can help kids experience success. For younger kids, choose games where everyone is a winner. Older kids benefit from more challenge.
- **Kids have short attention spans.** A good rule of thumb for estimating a child's attention span is no more than one minute per year of life. A 6-year-old would be able to concentrate for no more than six minutes on one activity.
- **Kids need for learning to be fun.** Kids are more likely to remember truths that are reinforced through activities. Choose fun activities that are age-appropriate. Remember that activities thrilling to a kindergartner will be boring to a sixth grader and vice versa.
- **Kids are curious.** Younger preschoolers use all their senses to explore the world around them. As children grow older, their curiosity remains, and they continue to want to know the how and why.
- **Kids are creative.** Kids can see the world differently than adults. Give a young child a box, and it becomes a spaceship or a castle. Older kids often express their creativity through music, games, and art.

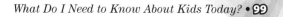

- **Kids are sensitive.** Though kids may not verbalize their feelings, they can read the emotions of those around them. Kids respond to the feelings expressed by the adults who care for them and teach them.

## What do kids need?
- **Love**—Children learn to express love when they experience love.
- **Trust**—Consistency in relationships builds trust.
- **Acceptance**—Unconditional love from parents and other adults lets kids know they are worthy and loved by God.
- **Independence**—Through choices, children can discover the gifts and talents God has given them.
- **Freedom**—Kids need the freedom to succeed and to fail. Learning to make right choices leads to self-discipline.
- **Security**—Providing an environment where kids feel safe and free from harm encourages an atmosphere for learning about God's plan.
- **Guidance**—Kids want adults to set limits and give direction. As kids grow older, and especially as they become preteens, their limits need to be expanded so they can learn to make right choices.
- **Accomplishment**—Provide opportunities for children to succeed, to learn new skills, and to develop their talents.

## What do I need to know about brain development?
Thinking is using one's mind to produce thoughts, to conceive and form ideas, and to allow those ideas to enter the mind. As kids learn to think, they develop perspective or a worldview on which they base their thoughts and decisions. Learning to think critically and creatively gives kids a tool to deal with today's information-based, high-tech society.

Cognition, the act of knowing, develops along a predictable time line. The capacity to think, absorb information, and take action in the world starts in the first months of life. At birth, a baby possesses only reflex actions but quickly develops basic skills such as putting food in his month.

Between the ages of two and seven, a child learns to identify objects, use body language, draw cause and effect conclusions, and verbalize his needs. A child sees a problem, creates a solution, and tries it out. This information helps him develop ways to see and understand the world. The peak of cognitive development, abstract thinking, develops as the prefrontal and frontal cortex matures. Abstract thinking is used in tasks such as weighing evidence, generating possibilities, identifying mistakes, and sequencing events. The preteen brain experiences a reshaping and reorganizing which accounts for the risk-taking and impulsive behavior. The frontal cortex is not fully mature until age 20 or older.

The brain's most important work is thinking and problem solving. Problem solving creates an explosion of brain activity causing connections to form, neurotransmitters to activate, and blood flow to increase. The most effective way to teach thinking skills is to incorporate real-world problems because the brain thrives on meaning, not on random information. Problem solving makes thinking meaningful. The brain, when faced with relevant, challenging conditions, excels in learning. Often teachers examine the facts of a Bible story but fail to discuss or connect the information to real-life, practical circumstances of the child.

## How do kids develop?

We can understand how children develop by looking at how Jesus grew in Luke 2:52. This verse shows us that kids grow mentally, physically, spiritually, and socially/emotionally.

## How do kids grow mentally?
> being curious and continually learning
> making choices
> learning language daily
> being creative and innovative
> beginning to focus for longer periods of time
> desiring to make independent decisions

## How do kids grow physically?
> moving from using only reflexes to developing fine motor skills
> using their whole body to learn
> experiencing uneven growth spurts
> needing rest or down time

## How do kids grow spiritually?
> developing a sense of trust
> moving from making simple choices to more complex ones
> learning to pray
> beginning to know right from wrong
> seeking to know God through studying the Bible

## How do kids grow socially?
> playing and working in groups

- developing friendships
- showing empathy
- showing interest in others' needs
- beginning to understand rules
- being loyal to family and friends

## How do kids grow emotionally?
- seeking affirmation from those around them
- looking for the familiar and shying away from change
- gaining confidence in their abilities
- expressing feelings openly and often loudly
- being shy and anxious in large groups of strangers
- becoming critical of their limitations and, as preteens, comparing themselves to others
- becoming critical of others

## How do kids approach learning?
Everyone approaches learning in different ways. Some people learn best through reading the instructions; others learn best by seeing a picture; others by feeling; and yet others by moving and doing. In recent years, we have learned that there are eight basic approaches to learning:

- **Logical**—Logical learners like to solve puzzles, find out how things are put together, and enjoy math. They enjoy problem solving, questions, and brain teasers. These kids like order and schedules.
- **Musical**—Musical learners hear music in everything. When music is playing in the room, they instinctively move to the beat without realizing it. They will often express themselves through music by making up songs, tapping out the beat, and making up raps.
- **Natural**—Natural learners thrive in the outdoors. They are in tune with God's creation. They are fascinated with plants and animals. They are highly interested in caring for the world.
- **Physical**—Kids love to move and are often in a state of constant movement. However, some kids need to move and use their whole body in order to learn. These kids may be able to multi-task easier than other kids because they are always in motion. They prefer hands-on projects, crafts, and service and mission projects.
- **Reflective**—Kids need time to be alone, but reflective learners need more. They understand who they are and how they feel. They love to sit alone and work on a project, read, and watch others. They will have one or two close friends that share a common interest or hobby.
- **Relational**—Kids are social, but some kids make friends more easily

than others. Relational learners love group activities. They are in tune with how others feel and what motivates them. They love to be in charge and direct the groups. In other words, they are the social networkers. As preteens, relational learners are the first to have a cell phone, a computer, and a social network Web site.

- **Verbal**—Kids who are verbal learners love words and have a command of vocabulary at an early age. They like to read, listen, and write and can clearly express ideas verbally.
- **Visual**—Seeing is believing, and visual learners see patterns in the world around them. They can see patterns in a concrete walkway when others just see concrete, and they see pictures in their heads when they hear a Bible story. Visual learners use their imaginations and creativity to make the world a better place.

### Why do boys and girls learn differently?

The major difference between the behavior and actions of boys and girls lies within the skull. The brain is the center of activity for the growth, development, and information processing of the human body. Hormones that influence the development of the embryo also guide the growth and development of the brain. Three major hormones affect the development and processing ability of the brain: estrogen, progesterone, and testosterone. Each chemical has its own special effect on the brain.

From the beginning of time, God has created human life through the same process. Chemicals are a necessary part growth. Estrogen and progesterone are responsible for mood stability, thought processes, perception, memory, personal motivation, intimacy, appetite, and the handling of stress. Testosterone, present at some level in boys and girls, is the dominant chemical responsible for the development of the male brain. This chemical is responsible for the aggressive nature inherent in boys.

The male brain is on average 10 percent larger than the female brain. Even though the brain is larger, because of chemical influences the boy's brain is a less efficient processor than a girl's brain.

While the male brain is 10 percent larger, it has a smaller corpus callosum. This connective tissue between the two hemispheres of the brain allows for cross talk between the two brain halves. Because this area is smaller, boys are at a disadvantage when verbalizing emotions and receiving and processing sensory information. Girls have better-developed language skills and also have better-developed senses of smell, hearing, sight, sense taste, and touch. What does this mean? This means only that boys have to process this information in a different and sometimes more lengthy process. Understanding these differences should affect the way you teach.

## What do I need to remember about boys?

- Boys can be outrageous.
- Boys like games.
- Boys like to ask silly questions.
- Boys like to ask serious questions.
- Boys like drama.
- Boys do like crafts.
- Boys don't sit still.
- Bribes do work.
- Boys like to know the goal.
- Boys may not act like they are listening, but they are.
- Boys like to chat.
- Boys really like male teachers.

## How do I keep boys interested in Bible study?

- Provide appropriate choices.
- Make learning a game.
- Use technology.
- Allow opportunities for appropriate humor.
- Provide male role models.
- Build good relationships.
- Provide activities that are meaningful to them.
- Create opportunities to move.
- Provide encouragement for things they do well.
- Provide hands-on learning experiences.

## What do I need to remember about girls?

- Girls like to talk.
- Girls can express their feelings but may keep them inside.
- Girls like to feel that they are part of a community.
- Girls are self-conscious of body image.
- Girls love hands-on projects.
- Girls can be silly.
- Girls are sensitive.
- Girls grasp the abstract faster than boys.
- Girls want to please adults.
- Girls do like games and competition.

## How do I keep girls interested in Bible study?

- ➤ Provide for time to build a relationship with girls.
- ➤ Work in small groups as often as possible.
- ➤ Talk to the girls while they are working.
- ➤ Listen to what the girls are talking about and relate Bible truths to their everyday lives.
- ➤ Use crafts and art projects when appropriate.
- ➤ Provide good female role models.
- ➤ Stay in touch with the girls.
- ➤ Use Bible stories that deal with relationships that can apply to life.

## How do I keep current with kids?

Children are exposed to images, sounds, and knowledge at earlier ages. The comfort level of using technology is almost inborn with kids. So once again you begin to ask yourself, "How do I keep up?"

- ➤ Learn to message using cell phones and the Internet.
- ➤ Learn how to use other forms of new technology.
- ➤ View shows kids are watching on TV.
- ➤ Read the books that kids are interested in.
- ➤ Learn about kids' favorite sports.
- ➤ Read a teen magazine.
- ➤ Use the Internet to learn what kids are interested in.
- ➤ Sit and talk to the kids you teach each week.
- ➤ Build relationships with the kids.

Kids today literally have the world at their fingertips and technologically will surpass the adults around them. However, they still long for one-on-one relationships with parents, teachers, and peers. We can provide the most up-to-date technology and the wildest activities at church, but in it all, we must make every effort to provide times to model our personal relationship with Christ by building relationships with kids.

*Cindy Lumpkin, Tim Pollard, and Mary Ann Bradberry*

*For more information the characteristics of kids,
check out the following items on the Kids Ministry 101 CD-ROM:*
"Characteristics of Preschoolers and Children," Item 32
"Do Babies Matter?" Item 33

# Chapter 25

# What Are Transitional Years?

*Oh listen, dear child—become wise; point your life in the right direction.*
*Proverbs 23:19 (The Message)*

Transitional years in kids' lives are those years when preschoolers and children either move to a new school and/or have tremendous physical and mental growth. In most churches the two most prominent transitional years are the kindergarten year and the preteen years.

## Why is the kindergarten year transitional?

During the kindergarten year, young children transcend from being preschoolers to school-age children. Nationwide, school districts are developing academic based, all-day kindergarten programs. For a kindergartner these changes are dramatic. Church programs for kindergartners must include age-appropriate Bible study and activities that the kids find enjoyable and engaging.

## What is a kindergartner?

- Kindergartners are the group of kids whom everyone wants to watch during the children's sermon. An insatiable quest for knowledge has left them with an almost unlimited number of questions. They are growing mentally as fast as they are physically.
- A child generally enters kindergarten when he is five years old.
- Kindergartners are at a unique learning level, needing both educational stimulation and time for free play.
- A kindergarten classroom evolves quickly from one similar to that of a preschool to one with a more elementary feel.

## What do kindergartners need socially?

- While kindergartners may begin the year timid or shy, they often turn into social butterflies tending to have several "best" friends.
- Due to the social nature of kindergartners, teachers of this age group are often remembered as being the child's favorite.
- Family is still a central focus of this age group.
- Kindergartners become aware of their *girlness* or *boyness* and tend to play in gender specific groups.
- Kindergartners have a strong desire to fit in with their peers.

## Why do some kindergartners seem so advanced?

> Traditionally, kindergarten would be considered a child's formal introduction to basic learning such as the alphabet, counting, color identification, and so forth.

> Formal education often begins with a child attending preschool where he learns most basic skills formerly taught in kindergarten.

> Depending on the rigidity of the preschool and the amount of time invested by parents for such things, some kindergartners may be reading when they enter school.

> A teacher's ability to recognize the child's educational level can help both the teacher and the child have an enjoyable classroom experience.

## How can I emotionally support kindergartners?

> Since they are learning new skills daily, kindergartners need praise and support in order to continue sharpening their abilities.

> A kindergartner may become frustrated easily if she doesn't understand a new concept or if she can't accomplish a physical feat that her peers can.

> Allow kindergartners time to talk openly about things on their minds such as fears, failures, or goals.

## How do I effectively guide classroom behavior of kindergartners?

> They are developing a deeper understanding of right and wrong.

> Rules and expectations for behavior should be brief, stated simply and in positive language, and clearly explained.

> Understanding that self-control is still developing, temper your expectations with the idea that frequent reminders of expected behavior will be necessary.

> Routines are important, so sticking to a schedule and a set pattern of structure and play are important.

## How do kindergartners learn?

> In a word, movement! Kindergartners are very active learners and function best in a classroom full of Bible-learning centers.

> Learning through playtime, dress-up, and exploration are fun and meaningful ways that kindergartners learn.

> Kindergartners also learn through observation or modeling. They will copy their older siblings and friends.

> Encourage active learning by providing opportunities to cook,

draw, build, and create.
> Avoiding strict structure and the use of too many worksheets will support a child's imaginative learning.

Kindergartners are wonderful little humans that are a joy to watch and teach. Their minds are like light bulbs just waiting to be turned on. Take the opportunity to make the most of the kindergarten year by encouraging learning, fostering strong relationships, and instilling confidence.

## Why are the preteen years transitional?

Preteens: just the very word may make your skin crawl. Preteens aren't really that scary; you just have to know how to deal with them. Part of what makes a preteen so annoying sometimes is also what makes him unique. Learning to love preteens for who they are—not who they were or who they are going to be—can take time. Getting to know them can be a rewarding experience for both you and your preteens.

## What is a preteen?

> A preteen is anyone who is in the fifth or sixth grade. This is usually in the 10- to 12-year-old age range.
> Preteens are often called *tweens, preadolescents,* or *tweenagers.*

## Why are preteens so emotional?

> Preteens are often emotionally volatile due to this time of rapid growth and physical maturation.
> Puberty is a time in a boy's or a girl's life when his or her body is undergoing the development of sexual organs. Because of the rapid buildup and release of hormones—unpredictable mood changes, aggressive behavior, and even depression can occur.
> Not all boys and girls enter puberty at the same time.
> Boys tend to hide their emotions as much as possible. A preteen boy might start crying or even fighting over a slight misstep by a peer. This may happen because preteen boys hide so much of their emotions that they reach a breaking point and must release them.

## How do you deal with emotional preteens?

> While emotional outbursts are understandable among preteens, establish an expectation of appropriate behavior.
> Never allow preteens to use violence against themselves or other preteens as a reaction to a perceived wrong.
> Remove the preteen from the situation and allow him time to cool off. Refrain from using the term "time out."

- Boys respond best to male teachers and girls to female teachers.
- Give a preteen time to express himself appropriately if he gets upset. Often this will help him to realize the bigger issue at hand.
- If a preteen uses aggressive behavior, discuss the issue with him. Then talk about the consequences of his actions. Consider meeting with the preteen and his parents to discuss the issue and to decide on disciplinary action.
- Sometimes behavior is a result of abuse. If you suspect abuse, you are legally obligated to report it. (See Chapter 9 for a discussion of legal issues and responsibilities.)

## What makes a preteen so active?

- Hormones! Preteens are stuck between childhood and adolescence.
- Preteens desire to be grown-up. While a preteen's physical characteristics may resemble that of her older peers, her mental maturity is still childlike.
- When planning Sunday School and discipleship sessions, retreats, and/or camps, remember that preteens will respond best to lessons that are active. Lecture teaching does not allow preteens to absorb much information. Active learning promotes better retention.

## What do preteens like?

- **Video games**—Preteens enjoy all types of video games. Boys tend to prefer action-oriented games, while girls tend to steer towards performance-based games.
- **Extracurricular activities**—Remember that not all boys enjoy sports, and not all girls enjoy makeup. This is especially true of preteens. Look for opportunities that will engage all of your preteens.
- **Friends**—Preteens want opportunities to be with their friends whether at church, school, or camp.

You can minister to preteens by providing a place at your church that they can call their own. Consider starting a preteen ministry where preteens can have a special place to talk openly, spend time with friends, and learn about God in a way they learn best.

*Kathy Collins and Jeff Land*

# Chapter 26
# How Do I Guide Kids to God?

Children grow physically in direct proportion to the nutritious food they eat and the emotional support they receive. Children grow spiritually in a similar fashion. They need to be immersed in an environment where God and His works are a part of everyday conversation. Kids need to hear Bible stories and Bible story conversation often. Deuteronomy 6:4-7 reminds us that it is the parents' primary responsibility to pass along their faith to their children by talking about God's Word, "When you sit in your house, and when you walk along the road, when you lie down and when you get up." That pretty much encompasses every waking moment of the day.

Children absorb what they see and hear—both the good and the bad. God's plan is that kids' environments be rich with opportunities to hear about God's teachings, to learn and know the foundational truths in Scripture, and to begin to put into practice what they learn from the Word.

Just as Jesus' growth is described in Luke 2:52, God has wired children to grow, "In wisdom and stature, and in favor with God and people." This favor with God occurs not just as kids listen to Bible stories but also as their experiences in life are enriched with truths and reminders about God and His love for them. As children watch the significant adults in their lives, they begin to form mental and emotional understandings of God. To understand God's unconditional love more readily, it is mandatory that children experience unconditional love in their homes and churches.

Parents and teachers need to remember a basic truth: for children to trust and believe in a God they cannot see they first must trust and believe in the adults they can see, hear, and touch. A child's sense of trust is developed by the age of three. By that age, a child begins to associate his feelings of trust or distrust with what he hears others say and teach about Jesus. If a child can trust his parents and teachers to keep promises and provide emotional stability, it is much easier for him to believe what that person teaches about God and His love.

A child's spiritual growth occurs in bits and pieces—as she hears songs about God and Jesus, listens to Bible stories and their truths, and sees those truths making a difference in the lives of her parents and other significant adults. She begins to equate the warm feelings of unconditional love with the type of love God has for her.

## What spiritual concepts or doctrine do children need to know?

Since the beginnings of Christian education, several foundational truths have been established as the support structure of faith development.

- **God**
- **Jesus**
- **Bible**
- **Creation**
- **Family**
- **Self**
- **Church**
- **Community & World**
- **Holy Spirit (grades 1–6)**
- **Salvation (grades 1–6)**

The *Levels of Biblical Learning*™ chart lists Bible truths in each of these concept areas that children need to hear repeatedly. Kids learn through repetition and begin to understand the ways Bible truths can make a difference in their lives. Babies hear very basic biblical truths. As kids grow and learn, their knowledge of biblical truths is built precept upon precept. By the preteen years, children will have heard all of the foundational truths. They will have developed and personalized a biblical worldview that enables them to see the events of life through the lens of "what does the Bible teach about this?"

## How do children learn about God, Jesus, and other biblical concepts at certain ages?

The *Levels of Biblical Learning*™ charts the natural progression of spiritual growth and development. Obviously, kids are unique and learn and grow at different rates. The chart provides a challenging road map for parents and teachers to provide an environment which gives children opportunities to hear God's Word, know God's Word, and do God's Word. Most of this learning occurs as parents and teachers share Bible stories and personal experiences, sing songs, and explain what the Bible teaches about God and His love for all people.

## How do I measure children's spiritual growth?

Adults discern how much children are learning about God's plan for their lives as they carry on conversations about Bible truths. Concerned teachers and parents ask open-ended questions that cannot be answered simply with a "yes" or a "no." For example, to evaluate what a child has learned about Jesus it would be better to say, "Tell me about some things the Bible teaches about Jesus," rather than the unproductive question, "Do you love Jesus?" Sharing one's faith with kids occurs as adults …

- carry on conversations with children about their faith rather than only sharing with children in a confrontational approach;
- observe kids' actions with family members, playmates, and friends;
- remain alert to kids' responses to activities and worship.

## What do I teach about salvation and when?

Preschoolers learn first that Jesus is their friend. As kids grow older and listen to teachings about Jesus and His ministry, they begin to hear words such as *Savior* and *Lord*. Adults should use child-friendly language when talking with children about Bible truths. All preschoolers and most younger children are concrete thinkers. They can only understand truths as they relate to what they have actually experienced. Kids do not have the ability to think symbolically like adults.

Kindergartners are usually ready to hear about Jesus' death on the cross, without the inclusion of graphic details. Kids will begin to make the connection that Jesus died on the cross because of people's sins. Help children understand that sins are unwise choices—disobedience to God.

The Bible never references age when it comes to salvation. Rather, the Bible teaches salvation as it relates to accountability. Children arrive at the point of accountability at different times. Usually, when a child is under conviction about the need to be forgiven of sin and to develop a personal relationship with God, she will ask questions related to becoming a Christian. Most of the time this conversation will be more than just the simple questions such as, "When can I get baptized?" and "When can I take the Lord's Supper?" When a child reaches the point of accountability and conviction by the Holy Spirit, involve the child in conversation and ask questions such as the following:

- What is sin?
- Who is Jesus?
- What did Jesus do?
- Why did Jesus come to earth?

> ➤ Why should you become a Christian?
> ➤ How can you accept Jesus as your Savior and Lord?

## Why is leading kids to take the first steps toward faith the most rewarding aspect of your job?

At church, you have the opportunity to help kids begin their spiritual journeys by explaining to them how to accept Jesus Christ as their Savior and Lord.

- **Pray.** Leading a child to Christ is a privilege, a joy, and an awesome responsibility! Begin your preparation by praying for every child you will encounter at church. No matter what your leadership position is at church, ask God to help you serve with a sweet, loving spirit and to make you sensitive to the needs of the boys and girls who come across your path. Other things to pray about include the following:
  - ➤ Ask God to make Himself real to the children.
  - ➤ Ask God to help you know how to talk with a child who approaches you with questions.
  - ➤ Ask God to prepare each child to respond when the Holy Spirit leads him to ask Jesus to be his Savior.
- **Build relationships.** Most people ask Jesus to be their Savior because they have developed a friendship with a Christian. Build relationships with the children you teach.
  - ➤ Get to know each child and call her by name.
  - ➤ Give buddy-hugs, pats on the back, high fives, and other appropriate touches.
  - ➤ Listen and show genuine interest in what a child shares.
  - ➤ Observe each child in action. Know what she likes and dislikes. Learn about her family, pets, interests, and talents.
- **Allow the Holy Spirit to lead.** As much as you may like to do so, you cannot make a child accept Jesus. Only God can draw children to Himself (John 6:44). There are some things you can do to prepare children to respond to the Holy Spirit's movement:
  - ➤ Continue to grow in your own spiritual life through faithful prayer and Bible study.
  - ➤ Pray for the children to respond to the Holy Spirit's leading.
  - ➤ Share the plan of salvation in clear, understandable terms.
  - ➤ Answer children's questions simply and honestly.
- **Answer questions as they arise.** Children are full of questions. Sometimes questions arise from a simple desire to know more about a topic and sometimes as a result of hearing information they do not understand. In any case, answering children's questions is an

important part of helping them learn about becoming a Christian. Here are a few tips to guide you in answering kids' questions:

- Ask follow-up questions. When a child asks a question, he often does not know exactly what to ask. Get clarification before deciding how to answer. For example, you might say: "Tell me more about what you are thinking." Or you may ask: "What made you ask that question? Where did you hear about this?" Remember, the question a child asks may not be his actual question. Also, a child may struggle with putting his questions into words adults can understand. Avoid asking questions that can be answered with "yes" or "no."

- Avoid giving more information than a child needs. Adults can be tempted to tell all they know on a subject. When a child asks a question, only answer what the child is asking. If the child wants more information, she will ask more questions. Asking questions allows her to gain information, correct misconceptions, and gain new insights.

- Do not jump to conclusions. A child may ask: "Why did Andy get baptized?" This question may be only a request for information, not a request for a gospel presentation. A child incorporates concepts and information over time.

- Speak in clear terms. Avoid symbolic analogies that may distract from discussion and understanding.

## How do I talk with children about becoming a Christian?

All parents and teachers need to develop skills in talking with children about becoming a Christian. A step-by-step approach is described in *Leading a Child/Friend to Christ Training Pack* which can be ordered online at *www.lifeway.com*. This pack includes not only tracts that share the gospel, but also a PowerPoint® presentation and a teaching plan to help train adults to conversationally talk with kids about becoming a Christian. Also included in the pack is a teaching plan to help equip older children in sharing their faith with friends. Two videos show adults and older children how to share their faith by using these resources. Still another feature in the training pack is a learner guide for both adults and older children with a keepsake copy of the Gospel that can be removed and placed in a Bible.

## What are tips for talking with kids about becoming a Christian?

- Ask open-ended questions. Children can often tell by the inflection of your voice what the answer to a "yes" or a "no" question is supposed to be. Open-ended questions help a child open up his

> heart and mind to you.
> ➤ Remain conversational, not confrontational.
> ➤ Avoid symbolic language.
> ➤ Make the distinction between becoming a Christian and being baptized and taking the Lord's Supper.
> ➤ Encourage the child to answer the questions.
> ➤ Re-phrase a question if a child cannot come up with an answer.
> ➤ Allow the child time to think about his answer.
> ➤ Avoid the temptation to state the answer yourself if a child does not immediately give an answer.
> ➤ Use a Bible translation that is comfortable for you and the child.
> ➤ Encourage the child to write down information about when, where, and how he became a Christian; what he prayed; and what he knows that God did because of what he prayed. Guide the child to date and sign this anchor statement.

## What do I do after a child becomes a Christian?

Offer a New Christians Class to affirm and encourage new believers. During the class, help children journal their experience of becoming a Christian. Give them immediate affirmation and help them "anchor" their decision. The journal will provide kids assurance of their salvation if they have doubts and questions later about the validity of their decision to follow Christ. A great resource for conducting a New Christians Class is *I'm a Christian Now, Revised* that can be ordered online at *www.lifeway.com/kids*.

Once a child becomes a Christian, he or she may develop a sense of urgency in telling friends about Jesus. An excellent way to follow up on this is to offer a Leading a Friend to Christ class for older children. This time with other kids can help each child journal his experience of becoming a Christian and also develop a prayer list of friends and family members who need to learn about Jesus. A teaching plan and a training video to use with this experience can be found in the *Leading a Child to Christ* training module available online at *www.lifeway.com/kids*.

## How do I teach about baptism and the Lord's Supper?

When children become Christians, they are excited about participating in baptism and the Lord's Supper. Help kids understand that these two ordinances are different steps to take *after* becoming a Christian. Jesus set an example by being baptized and encouraged all believers to be baptized to show others they have trusted Him as their Savior. Explain also that baptism symbolizes Jesus' death on the cross, His burial in the tomb, and

God's raising Him from the dead to become the Savior of the world. Teach about these ordinances in further detail during the New Christians Class, and encourage kids to participate in a congregational worship service where they can view a baptism and the observance of the Lord's Supper.

## Why is Bible memory important?

Learning and committing to memory key Bible verses is a critical element in the lives of all believers. Memorized verses provide assurance of God's grace, love, and faithfulness. The Bible says: "I have treasured Your word in my heart so that I may not sin against You" (Psalm 119:11). Memorizing God's Word and internalizing its truths can guide and change behavior which is an important part of a young believer's spiritual growth. Just learning the words of the Bible is valuable. However, the critical added value occurs when a child understands the words and teachings of Bible verses and applies them to her life situations.

## How do children learn Bible skills?

Kids do not learn Bible skills accidentally. Loving and caring teachers and parents provide hands-on opportunities for kids to learn to use the Bible. Bible skills activities can take place in Bible study sessions, discipleship experiences, Bible drill, and during family time at home. Tuned-in teachers provide Bible skills games and songs that make developing Bible skills fun and exciting. As kids learn to handle the Bible proficiently, they are more likely to read it on a regular basis. Tangible resources, such as devotional guides, help children develop the discipline of a daily quiet time of Bible reading and prayer. The curriculum that kids ministry leaders choose should always include opportunities for Bible skills development.

## How do I teach about prayer?

Children learn about prayer by watching and listening to the significant adults in their lives as they pray. If prayer is important to their teachers and parents, prayer will become an important part of children's lives, too. It is very important that children begin to feel comfortable just thinking about how much they love God and how thankful they are for what God has done for them.

- ➤ Kids need to learn they can pray anytime and anywhere.
- ➤ Children begin to pray with memorized prayers. Do not criticize a child for repeating someone else's words.
- ➤ Caring adults can help kids understand that they can talk with God just as they can talk to friends and family members.

- Kids will begin to understand that they can be honest with God and share exactly what they are thinking and feeling—even the emotions of anger and fear.
- Most children will begin to develop a feeling of awe and wonder that they can actually carry on a conversation God.

## How do I involve kids in ministry?

Many Bible study teachers emphasize learning facts and truths from the Bible. However, insightful parents and teachers will be eager to give opportunities for children to actually put Bible truths into practice. It is much more meaningful for a child to help prepare and deliver a basket of food to a needy family or someone who is sick rather than simply to color a picture of someone visiting a sick person. Plan ministry experiences that are age-appropriate and that will help kids apply the Bible truths they are learning. Many churches are making ministry opportunities part of their curriculum. These include projects for a class of children, times for families to travel and minister together, or something as simple as making cards or writing notes of encouragement to shut-ins. Whatever path you choose to take in this endeavor, each child needs to develop a sense of "doing" what God has asked each believer to do: show love to others.

An excellent way to get children more in tune with ministry is to offer them learning sessions about stewardship. Children then become aware that not only can they give their money to their church to further its ministry, but they can offer their time and abilities to be used in God's service. Six free sessions on stewardship are offered online at *www.lifeway.com/kidsstewardship.*

*Jerry Vogel*

*For more information on biblical concepts and Bible skills for kids ministry, check out the following items on the Kids Ministry 101 CD-ROM:*
"Levels of Biblical Learning," Item 2
"Levels of Bible Skills," Item 3

# Chapter 27
# How Do I Create a Relevant and Fun Ministry?

*Can you translate: "r u oot"?*

## Am I relevant?

Take a minute to answer the following questions as they relate to your childhood. Record the first thought that comes to your mind.

1. What type of video game system did you play?
2. What was your favorite video game?
3. What was your favorite music group?
4. Did you wear bell-bottoms the first time they were popular?
5. What did your first cell phone look like?
6. What was your favorite television show?
7. Can you translate: "r u oot"?

## Let's see how you did.

1. If you answered Atari®, Nintendo®, or Sega®, you could be in danger of being outdated by your kids. The Nintendo is still around, but now it has several initials beside each system such as Wii™ or DS™. Keeping up with the latest video gaming system will help you as your look for ideas for retreats and camps. You can design games and activities around gaming scenarios. Boys and girls love video games!

2. If you answered Pong, Frogger, or Super Mario Brothers, watch out! Video games are now 3-D, action-packed adventures. Kids can even text each other through video games. Video games are no longer played with a joystick; they involve the player's entire body! Your children's ministry must involve active movement if it is going to be appealing to children. Think about it like this: your ministry is competing with the entertaining world of video games.

3. Did you say New Kids on the Block or The Beatles? Musicians come and go these days. You must be able to recognize to whom the kids are listening. With television shows designed to make average people superstars overnight, kids today may have a distorted view of reality. On the flip side, because of the growing popularity of MP3 players, kids demand quality music. Are you still trying to make kids sing the same old songs? Be on the lookout for fresh, new Christian CDs and videos.

4. If yes, you are in luck! Have you noticed that fashion has come back around to old styles? The only issue is these newly styled versions of clothing are often too short and too revealing! As a children's worker, you have the opportunity to influence boys and girls to dress appropriately. This has much to do with the way you dress yourself.

5. If your first cell phone came in a briefcase, you are no doubt amazed at how much smaller they are today. The point is not that cell phones are smaller. The point is that kids use hundreds, if not thousands, of dollars worth of technology each day. This provides a direct implication to your ministry. Using technology in your ministry can capture the interest of the kids!

6. *Andy Griffith, Saved By the Bell,* and *Happy Days* might qualify as favorite television shows for some of you reading this. However, many of the kids in your ministry have never even heard of these shows! If you have watched a modern cartoon, you have no doubt noticed that they are very different from the *Flintstones*. When media is used in your ministry, be careful to choose only the best resources that are biblically accurate, relevant, and well-produced so kids will find them appealing. Using media in your ministry is very important. However, you will find that the use of mediocre media is quite ineffective.

7. Think about it! Wasn't it nice, back in the good old days, when people wrote in sentences? Were you able to translate the text message above? *Are you out of touch?* Kids communicate in their own language these days. The words you used, such as *radical* and *far out* have been replaced with much *hipper* lingo. Think about the way you relate to the kids in your ministry. Keeping up-to-date with modern forms of communication will help you stay connected to the kids in your ministry.

**How can you take what you know about kids today and apply it to your ministry to create a fun and vibrant place where children want to come?**
- **You must make a conscious effort to keep current.**
  - ➤ Subscribe to magazines targeted at children.
  - ➤ Watch television shows kids are watching. Remember, they are not only watching Disney® or Nickelodeon®. Your knowledge of both the good and the bad shows kids watch can help shape the way you minister to kids.
  - ➤ Listen to what your kids are saying and pay attention to what they are doing. You may be surprised at how much they already know.

- Watching television shows on channels that kids watch such as Disney, Nickolodeon, or Discovery Kids will increase your ability to speak *kid* fluently!
- **You must make your ministry biblically sound.**
    - It is really easy to get sucked into the cute, edgy, or even silly side of children's ministry. Avoid making this your primary focus.
    - Create a list of values and goals to guide how you choose curriculum for ministry. (See Chapter 18 on how to make wise curriculum choices.)
    - Your ministry is also your legacy. It is always great to be known as the fun-loving, hip kids leader. However, it is imperative that the kids who graduate from your ministry have developed a biblical worldview based on what they learned.
- **You must make your ministry appealing.**
    - Children's ministry can be a difficult task. Since most kids ministries are responsible for children from birth through sixth grade, consider developing several different age-specific ministries.
    - You must seek to meet the needs of kids.
    - Break your ministry into segments. Look at each ministry according to the age groups represented in the segments. Choose curriculum that is developed specifically for those age groups.
    - Enlist volunteers who are passionate about the areas in which you have enlisted them to serve. You do not want a preschool worker leading a preteen boys' Bible study!
- **You will use décor and color thoughtfully.**
    - There is nothing inherently wrong with the use of color on the walls of your children's ministry classrooms. There are colors, however, which cause adverse reactions in children. Search the Web for information regarding child-appropriate colors.
    - Consider carefully your decision to have permanent murals painted on the walls. Are the children in your church going to get tired of these pictures after a while? A cost-saving option would be life-size photos and posters that are readily available from a variety of companies. Those posters can be rotated or replaced periodically.
    - Becoming more interested in making your ministry area look pretty than developing a solid curriculum is a real danger. Don't get caught on the "cute train"!
- **You are not a failure if you don't have the latest, greatest, and newest of everything.**
    - At a point in your ministry funds may become tight. Strive to provide the best curriculum and resources within your budget.

- Enlist the talents of church members as often as possible. Chances are, there are people in your church who are capable of helping you create a dynamic children's space using technology, color, print, and media. Seek out these people and enlist their help in your ministry to kids.

- **You can become comfortable with the use of technology in kids ministry.**
  - Like it or not, technology is here to stay. You must become comfortable with the use of technology around kids. Your thoughtful use of technology will serve as a teaching tool for showing kids how it can be used effectively.
  - Work with your church's sound, media, and lighting volunteers to think of ways to use technology.
  - Consider asking church members to donate old computers for the creation of a computer lab. Kids will enjoy playing Bible-related computer games and memory verse activities.
  - Video clips are an interesting way to set the stage for discussion with kids. Provide the necessary equipment as needed.

- **You can plan fun, yet meaningful, events for kids.**
  - Enlist a team of volunteers to help each time you plan events for your kids ministry.
  - Try to incorporate meaning into the events that you plan. Add canned food drives, toy collections, and penny donations to almost any event to provide kids a way to support ministries in your community.
  - Fun service projects will attract kids and teach them about serving others.

*Jeff Land*

# Chapter 28
# How Do I Guide Behavior?

*But don't, dear friend, resent GOD'S discipline; don't sulk under his loving correction. It's the child he loves that GOD corrects; a father's delight is behind all this.*
*Proverbs 3:11-12 (The Message)*

If most of us are honest, one of the first ideas that comes to mind when thinking about guiding behavior and discipline is some type of negative reinforcement. The word *discipline* has come to mean "to punish or to bring under control." However, *discipline* and *disciple* originally come from the Latin word *disciplina* which means "to instruct or teach." Therefore, in its best sense, *to discipline* is "to guide or to lead by teaching."

### Is positive guidance and discipline biblical?
Consider the following passages of Scripture and their truths:
- **Psalm 94:12-13a:** Discipline brings happiness and protects one from troubled times.
- **Proverbs 3:11-12:** Just as God disciplines those He loves, we discipline those we love.
- **Proverbs 15:5,31-32:** It is wise to listen to correction, and it gives one good sense.
- **Hebrews 12:7-11:** Discipline can seem painful rather than enjoyable, but it results in peace and righteousness.

### How can I create an atmosphere of positive learning for kids?
Remember, without self-discipline and preparation, teachers are often the cause of behavior issues in their classes.
- **Know and understand kids.** They do not understand symbolic language and have short attention spans.
- **Pray for wisdom.** Pray before planning. Pray for kids and their families to help you see each child through the eyes of Jesus.
- **Plan ahead.** If you do not have a plan, the kids do. Once the kids' plan goes into action, it is difficult for even the best teachers to gain control of the group and teach effectively.
- **Prepare the environment.** Rooms with too much equipment can result in behavior challenges. Make sure the equipment in each room is safe, needed, and complements the age of the children.

## What are reasons kids misbehave?

- **Attention**—Some children misbehave to get attention. They are willing to risk correction in order to get attention from the significant adults in their lives. Look for positive behavior to affirm verbally.
- **Control**—Kids desire limits, they are constantly testing boundaries to see who is in control. Use statements such as: "I know you may get to do that in another classroom, but in Mr. Jerry's room, this is the rule."
- **Revenge**—Revenge is an innate response for children. "He hit me first!" Give simple, clear responses to such statements: "Even though someone hurts you, it does not give you the right to hurt him back. Use your words to tell your friend how you feel."
- **Inadequacy**—Another reason for misbehavior can be feelings of inadequacy. Often the "class clown" is choosing this type of behavior to cover up an inadequacy. Kids may feel inadequate because they are poor readers or are experiencing a difficult situation at home. At the moment a kid suspects that he may be "found out," he will choose to redirect attention and use misbehavior to accomplish this task.

## What are the principles for guiding children's behavior?

Obviously, your ultimate goal is to help each child develop self-discipline. Consider the following practical helps to achieve your goal.

- **Establish boundaries.** This may be as simple as defining the block area with tape or more complex such as having a rule about only using hands for kind gestures.
- **Maintain established boundaries consistently and fairly.** Children quickly sense a teacher's preferential treatment of one child.
- **Use positive, clear suggestions that at times include options.** Don't just say: "No," "Stop," or "I told you not to do that." Take the time to state choices of good behavior following the corrective statement: "You may do 'this' or 'this.' Which do you choose?"
- **Respect the child as a person.**
- **Plan and prepare with the children's interests in mind.** Resist your hesitation if an activity seems too messy. Kids love to participate in a messy activity, even if it results in cleaning up a mess.
- **Listen to a child when he talks.**
- **Be a positive role model.** If you don't want kids to sit on tables, you do not sit on tables.
- **Shift to a different activity if the group is restless.** Always have additional activities on hand.
- **Deal with problems immediately.** If one teacher is leading a group-time experience, she will need assistance in dealing with challenging

behavior. It may be as simple as the additional teacher moving closer in proximity to the disruptive child.
- **Plan for a variety of activities and projects to appeal to different types of learners.**
- **Identify the needs of children.** Are they hungry? bored? upset?

## What techniques can I use to correct unacceptable behavior?
- **Get the child's attention.** Make eye contact on her level. Use appropriate touch such as a gentle touch to a shoulder or a gentle, guiding hand to the chin. With older children, a simple statement like such as, "Let me see your eyes," will help develop eye contact.
- **Give only the directive you plan to enforce.** Omit idle threats.
- **Offer options to help redirect activity.** State what needs to be stopped. Give two possible choices of acceptable behavior.
- **Let the child know that you are on her side.** Even though you dislike the child's behavior, you still like her.
- **When you the finish the reprimand, it's over!**

## What are the steps to take in correcting unacceptable behavior?
- **Help the child understand the need to change his behavior.**
- **Remove the child from the group.** Place him at the perimeter of the room so that he can still see the fun going on within the group. Be sure peers cannot hear what you say to the disruptive child.
- **Remove the child.** Go out into the hallway for a talk.
- **Seek the advice of an authority figure.**
- **Schedule a parent conference.** Never talk in the doorway about behavior problems. State the challenge: "I love Angela. I am so glad that she is in our class. I want to be a good teacher for her. But I am having trouble knowing what to do when Angela does such and such. How do you deal with this behavior at home?"

Successfully guiding children's behavior requires good planning and a positive strategy to get results. The key to a quality learning environment is discipline on the part of the teachers and an understanding of how children are wired by God and how they learn.

*Jerry Vogel*

# Community?

## So it's not all about me?

**A**nn wanted to go to Vacation Bible School because the pastor had promised her a special treat. Her parents didn't want her to attend, but she insisted. Ann learned about Jesus, and she became a Christian. One day her mom asked why she was sad. Ann said, "I'll be in heaven, and you and dad won't." The day Ann was baptized, her mom, dad, and siblings became Christians. Years later, Ann was in a car accident and died. Her parents grieved for Ann, but they knew she was in heaven. Other family members became Christians after attending Ann's funeral and witnessing the love and care of the church for Ann's family. Later, Ann's mom and dad began to work in VBS to help girls and boys come to know Jesus like Ann had.

*Jerry Wooley*

Some people were even bringing infants to Him so He might touch them, but when the disciples saw it, they rebuked them. Jesus, however, invited them: "Let the little children come to Me, and don't stop them, because the kingdom of God belongs to such as these. I assure you: Whoever does not welcome the kingdom of God like a little child will never enter it."

*Luke 18:15-17*

# Chapter 29

# How Do I Reach My Community?

Building a bridge between the community and your church should be near the top of your "to do" list as a kids leader. However, too often this priority is pushed aside by day-to-day tasks that get in the way. Intentional planning for community outreach is essential, or it will never happen.

## How do I find prospects?

- **Vacation Bible School**—This is one of, if not *the* best, means for connecting with your community and finding prospects. Many times you minister only to the children within your church. While they are important, you miss the opportunity to build relationships with families outside the church. Good VBS registration and follow-up are crucial to making the most of your outreach efforts.

- **Large Events**—A fall festival, Christmas programs, and similar events can be great community relationship builders. The key to success in transforming them into true outreach events lies in good registration. Consider giving away a door prize and asking guests to register to win. In addition to name, address, phone number, and e-mail address, ask for permission to send information regarding your church's future events.

- **Adult Sunday School classes**—The parents of prospects for your kids ministry are prospects for your young and median adult classes. Work together with adult classes to discover names of families they are hoping to reach.

- **Cards from congregation**—Distribute "I know a family" cards to all adult classes to suggest names of unchurched families in the community with kids. Encourage them to include people they work with, live near, and come in contact with every day.

- **Parents Day Out and Weekday programs**—Programs such as these can be great bridge builders for your ministry. These families have already entrusted their children to your care. Go the next step and invite them to Sunday School or other events at your church.

- **Realtors**—Realtors often put together "Welcome to the Neighborhood" packets for newcomers to the community. Ask realtors in your church and community to include information about your church's ministries and upcoming events in the packets. If your church offers a Wednesday night meal, consider including a free "first time guest" ticket for the family.
- **LifeWay Prospect Services**—Services such as this go past finding just newcomers and can help you locate specific age-group prospects within your area to which you can target information about programs and events. For information on this service, go to *www.lifewaystores.com/prospectservices.*

## How do I reach new and expectant parents?

Consider such options as …

- **offering parenting classes** including topics such as potty training, positive discipline, nutrition, and the like.
- **placing parenting magazines with your church's label or card attached in pediatricians' and obstetricians' offices as well as at adoption agencies.**
- **watching newspapers for new baby announcements and sending a congratulatory note.** Include information about upcoming parenting classes your church offers.

## What events reach families?

As you contemplate what type of events to schedule, be sure you understand the needs of the families you're trying to reach. Today's parents are busy people and want to make the best use of their time. Keep in mind the following:

- **Restrict the time of your events** to under two hours because time is a precious commodity, and kids' attention spans are short.
- **Plan separate events for parents and kids at the same time.** For example, if a parenting class is offered, provide a fun, learning activity for the children.
- **Family time is precious.** To help keep the family together, schedule events that the whole family can participate in such as family picnics, gym time, and movie nights. Be sure to get a license before showing a movie. For licensing information, go to *www.cvli.com.*
- **Today's parents want to make a difference in the world around them.** Consider scheduling a night for your ministry to work in your church's food or clothing bank or bake cookies together to give to local community helpers.

- **Start a moms group.** Encourage moms to get together for fun, exchanging parenting tips, Bible study, and support. Keep in mind that you may need to offer alternate meeting times for moms who work outside the home. Provide child care if at all possible.
- **Take church to expecting parents who are prospects.** You may need to take the church to them! Consider setting up a water tent at a local sports complex on the weekend. Attach labels with your church's address to bottles of water and distribute them at next week's soccer games.

### How do I motivate people to actually follow up after an event?

All the outreach ideas in the world will just take up your precious time unless you have a plan in place to follow up with those prospects you've discovered.

- **Be intentional in planning.** Remember, if you fail to plan, then you plan to fail. For example, let your Vacation Bible School teachers know up front they will be asked to help contact visitors who attended VBS.
- **Simplify the process.** Show your leaders that you value their time. Provide postcards with names and addresses for kids workers to send a note to their prospects. Include postage!
- **Get help! Don't try to do it alone.** Observe teachers and others who have a natural gift to help people feel welcome. Ask them to serve on a ministry team that will schedule outreach events and follow-up.

*Klista Storts*

*For more information on outreach for your kids ministry,*
*check out the following items on the Kids Ministry 101 CD-ROM:*
"Ministry Organizational Chart," Item 34
"FIRST CONTACT," Item 35
"16 Ways to Say Welcome," Item 36

# Chapter 30
# Why Is Vacation Bible School So Important?

*Go, therefore, and make disciples of all nations, baptizing them in the name of the Father and of the Son and of the Holy Spirit, teaching them to observe everything I have commanded you. And remember, I am with you always, to the end of the age.*
*Matthew 28:19-20*

For over eight decades, Vacation Bible School has been synonymous with fruit punch, macaroni crafts, and a welcome break from the monotony of long, hot summers. But beyond these obvious reasons why VBS is important, VBS continues to be one of the most universally successful evangelistic outreach events.

Over three million people attend annually. Ten percent indicate they are not affiliated with a church or on-going Bible study. These 300,000 individuals and their families represent tremendous evangelistic opportunities, provided churches are committed to the follow-up efforts necessary to cultivate and enrich the relationships.

This help starts not with an activity or resource but with the decision by each church to make evangelism the primary purpose and result of VBS. Until this decision is intentional and put into practice, a church will never realize the full evangelistic impact VBS can have on individuals, the church, and the community.

Once this decision has been made, consider these tips to ensure your VBS is the evangelistic flagship event of the year.

- **Plan VBS with follow-up in mind.** Too often people see the week of VBS as the big event when, in reality, it is just a prelude to the real event—evangelistic follow-up opportunities.
- **Enlist a follow-up director.** Effective VBS follow-up requires creativity, organization, and someone to orchestrate the plans.
- **Establish a goal for the number of unchurched individuals you plan to register.** Start with the national average of 10 percent.
- **Make evangelism and follow-up the responsibility of every member of the VBS team and the church.** The pastor cannot conduct VBS alone and shouldn't be expected to conduct follow-up

alone. Enlist every VBS worker with the knowledge that participation in follow-up activities is expected.

- **Provide follow-up training.** While Christians have the greatest news of all to share, there is typically great fear in sharing it. Provide training in appropriate ways to make phone calls and home visits and to lead children and adults to Christ.

- **Connect VBS to Sunday School or an on-going Bible study ministry by recruiting leadership from all age groups to be on the follow-up team.** When a child attends VBS, she represents outreach opportunities for more than just the children's Sunday School. An important aspect of the initial follow-up contact should be the discovery of the family network. Once discovered, information should be passed on to other members of the follow-up team. The team should then invite each member of the family to the appropriate Bible study class and ministry opportunities.

- **Make initial follow-up assignments by the last day of VBS and ensure initial contacts are made immediately.** Valuable opportunities are lost when follow-up contacts are delayed for days or weeks.

- **Track follow-up assignments to ensure every contact is made.** Create a reporting system that requires team members to report back in a timely manner.

- **Create a plan to ensure multiple contacts during a three- to six-month period following VBS.** Include personal visits, phone calls, mailed information, e-mails, and invitations to other events and ministry opportunities.

- **Plan post VBS events designed to continue the VBS experience.** Create opportunities such as neighborhood Bible clubs, a VBS reunion, or fall festivals designed to bring together unchurched families with people they met during VBS.

- **Celebrate follow-up results with the congregation.** When appropriate, include testimonies from follow-up team members and individuals who made decisions as a result of VBS.

*Jerry Wooley*

*For a more information on planning Vacation Bible School,
check out the following item on the Kids Ministry 101 CD-ROM:
"Planning Vacation Bible School," Item 37*

# Chapter 31
# How Do I Plan Special Events?

*Rejoice in the Lord always. I will say it again: Rejoice! Philippians 4:4*

**"We need you to plan something for the kids."** Those nine little words often send leaders of children and preschoolers scrambling from the room like pilots after a mission briefing. So many churches are good at planning special events and emphases that exclude children. The list might include revivals, stewardship programs, capital campaigns, women's conferences, special speakers, church celebrations, meetings to deal with sensitive topics or issues, and home fellowships. Even events that are planned and sponsored by the kids ministry, such as parent conferences, sometimes require separate programming for children.

## Why are special events a challenge?
Special events present unique challenges, not the least of which is leadership. Many leaders want to participate in the special event instead of helping with the children's portion of the event. Other challenges include meeting the needs of a broad mix of age groups, the length of the program, unpredictable start and finish times, facilities, and of course, budget considerations.

## How do I plan a special event?
- **Begin with a good attitude.** Recognize the benefit of the larger event to your church and see yourself as a partner helping make greater participation possible. The special event may provide the opportunity to do something you have always wanted to do, but couldn't find the time or resources to do it, such as bringing in a special guest.
- **Connect kids to the main event.** As you plan, look for ways to help preschoolers and children connect to the larger event it supports. For example, if the adults are focusing on stewardship, take a few moments to talk with the kids about giving. Kids will enjoy your event much more and appreciate feeling part of the emphasis. You will have a fun event that provides spiritual focus for the kids while casting you as a team player, both of which are positives for your ministry.
- **Enlist leaders.** Finding leaders will often be one of your greatest challenges. Some churches swap leaders with other churches—you send adults to help me; I'll send adults to help you on a similar occasion. Either way, you will want to be sure to have one or two

people present who know your kids. Depending on the scope of the churchwide event, older youth or single adults may also be a leadership option. You might offer to pay them for their help so they can earn money for an upcoming youth event such as a summer mission trip.

- **Provide food.** You may be asked to provide a meal. Keep it fun, simple, and healthy. Consider serving fruit drinks and water instead of soft drinks.
- **Budget for resources.** Many special events are planned well in advance and become separate line items in the church budget. As plans unfold, don't hesitate to ask for resources for your event.
- **Develop clear drop-off, pickup, and reservation instructions.** Make sure the instructions are included in all event publicity. If the adults meet at a different site, pad your start and end times by about 30 minutes.
- **Decide on the type of event.** Beyond these general considerations and planning ideas, the main question still remains: What are you going to do? You will first need to decide whether to keep everyone together and plan programming that all ages can enjoy, or divide according to age levels and rotate among various stations. Number of children, number of leaders, and availability of facilities will play a part in that decision.
- **Invite a special guest.** Inviting a special children's entertainer (magician, juggler, ventriloquist, and so forth) to your event can be fun and can fill a large amount of the time. However, even the best of these folks will typically not want to be in front of your group for much more than one hour.
- **Plan activities.** Plan to begin and end with activities that children can join as they arrive and slip away from when their parents come to get them. Consider parachute play, games in an open gym or game room, viewing videos, inflatables (which can be rented), and music, especially songs with accompanying actions (such as LifeWay's VBS songs and *Worship KidStyle* music).
- **Take it on the road.** If the weather and time of year permit, you might want to take your special event outside or even on the road. Find a church member who has a farm, or head for a local park that has a ball field or a cool playground. Grill hot dogs and hamburgers for supper. Consider changing the rules to a group game like kickball to increase participation and decrease competition. Instead of playing three outs per inning, let everyone kick once each time a team bats or kicks. Players either score or make an out. Be sure to allow some free

time just for running and free play. To wind things down, build a fire and enjoy s'mores.

- **Consider a movie night.** Show a family friendly movie. Add popcorn and drinks, and you're set for at least an hour. Be sure your church has a license to show movies to groups. One licensing service, Church Video Licensing International, is available online at *www.cvli.com*.

*David Garrard*

*For additional ideas on planning special events,*
*check out the following items on the Kids Ministry 101 CD-ROM:*
"Ideas for Special Events for Children," Item 38
"Kids Retreats 101," Item 39
"Tips for Summer Planning," Item 40
"Day Camping in 9 Easy Steps," Item 41

# Chapter 32
# How Do I Build a Family Ministry?

*But if it doesn't please you to worship the LORD, choose for yourselves today the one you will worship: the gods your fathers worshiped beyond the Euphrates River, or the gods of the Amorites in whose land you are living. As for me and my family, we will worship the LORD. Joshua 24:15*

Because of your love for boys and girls and your realization that they belong to the Lord and to their parents, one of your joys is to partner with Him and their parents in ministry. It is impossible to fully affect kids' lives without involving and influencing their families' lives. Family ministry is the key to making a difference for the kids you serve.

God's Word is clear that parents are the primary faith providers for their children. One of the most important roles parents fill is that of transmitters of their faith in God, according to His design. There are, of course, deterrents to parents fulfilling their faith role. Parents can be affected by several factors:

- **Time Issues**—In today's busy world, families' schedules are in high tension. In order to provide time for faith involvement, parents must make wise choices about what to include or exclude from their lives and their children's lives.
- **Interest**—Though believing parents may desire faith connections for their children, many distractions can prevent this from being a priority. The temporal often takes precedence over the eternal because of the immediacy of the "here and now" concerns.
- **Awareness**—Many parents see the role of faith development as belonging to the church. They have outsourced this vital responsibility as they have other duties. Parents must become aware of and be convicted by God's plan which is clear in His Word.
- **Commitment**—Affecting a child's spiritual growth is a lifelong endeavor. It is often a challenge for parents to make and keep the commitment necessary for playing a long-term role in laying their child's faith foundations. The consistency and dedication needed for this to occur is a full-time commitment.

The lasting relationships necessary for family ministry to begin and grow become a reality as you make this area of your ministry a priority. Any human connectedness, which we call "relationship," requires willingness to make the time within your ministry for opportunities of togetherness. You must make yourself available and make your ministry accessible.

## What are the keys for connecting with families?

- **Provide a balanced,** multifaceted ministry, which addresses the social, emotional, spiritual, intellectual, and physical needs of families.
- **Stay in touch with the needs,** struggles and challenges of families.
- **Include relevant programs,** events, and ministries that align with the needs and concerns of the families.
- **Strengthen existing familial relationships.**
- **Understand the demographics of families in your community.**
- **Offer opportunities for families to connect with other families.**
- **Provide structures that attract homogenous groupings and involve a cross section of ages and life stages.** The network of support within the church family will become stronger.
- **Promote and encourage intergenerational participation and involvement,** as well as activities, which will build and strengthen individual family units.

## How do I provide a strong family ministry?

- **Start early.** It is never too early to begin the connections necessary to bond with parents. As soon as you know of a pregnancy, you can begin the process of inclusion in your ministry area. Host an "expectant parent" brunch or provide a "what to expect" evening. Including information and celebration for prospective parents starts the bond early. Young adults are open to input because of the newness of the experience and the feelings of being overwhelmed!
- **Start small.** There is no need to assume you must do everything from the beginning. Consider starting small, perhaps with a once-a-year event for parents and children. Such an event allows teachers to interact with families and is a good beginning. It can pay big dividends as you, your teachers, and the parents of the children you love and serve get to know each other better.
- **Start expanding.** As you become more confident with your family ministry, increase the number of ministries to parents. Plan for connections with parents to begin as the new Sunday School year begins. Offer additional opportunities during the holiday season, in the springtime, during Vacation Bible School, and other times that fit your church's schedule. Start the process to include those parents who are involved and to invite those who have not yet become connected.

- **Restart.** Be willing to restart. Ministry is made up of attempts! Try something! If it works, try it again—with a few adjustments made for things you learned the first time. If it doesn't work, try another type of connection. In developing a ministry with families, one of the biggest mistakes is not trying anything at all. Do not duplicate what others in your area are doing. Instead, plan specific, simple events that meet the needs of the families in your church and that can bring the families closer to one another, to their church, and to their Lord.

## What factors do I need to prioritize to connect with families?

In order to develop effective ministry to and with families, prioritize critical factors that will help parents build strong families. Encourage families in behaviors, such as the following. These areas can provide excellent topics for discussion groups or for parent sessions:

- **Effective communication**—Families improve when they are …
  - talking about deeper issues and topics.
  - discussing feelings, thoughts, experiences, and ideas rather than only focusing on actions.
  - expressing appreciation for one another.
- **Commitment to one another**—Families become stronger when they realize that …
  - commitment is the basic building block of any relationship.
  - parents cannot focus on self-fulfillment but instead must act on what is best for the whole family.
  - each parent must be committed to each family member as well as to the family unit itself.
  - setting priorities is essential in choosing among the many options available to the family.
- **Crisis resolution**—Critical for family relationships to survive is the necessity for …
  - dealing with the intense pressures all families face rather than ignoring them.
  - realizing that a crisis can pull a family apart or draw it together, based on the way it is handled.
  - being flexible and adapting to changing situations.
  - developing skills to handle crisis situations.
- **Religious commitment**—For children to grow spiritually, parents must …
  - commit to their own personal faith and spiritual growth.
  - realize that their religious beliefs have an impact on their children's lives and give them a sense of stability.

> acknowledge that the most critical element in a child's spiritual growth is not special programs, great teachers, or even a strong church. Instead, the single most important factor is the influence of the child's immediate family.

## How can you involve children's parents in their spiritual growth and provide ministry to their families?

Keep the end in mind—the desire to provide true ministry, not just activities, for families. You will affect the children's lives not just for today but also for eternity. To more effectively minister to families, try some of the following tips:

- **Work to develop a personal relationship with parents.**
- **Follow up quickly on all possible opportunities with parents,** such as answering their questions, responding to their requests for information, acknowledging and implementing (when prudent) their feedback on activities, and so forth.
- **Show that you truly care about children.** You win parents' hearts when they see that their child really matters to you.
- **Work together with your church's adult leadership to connect parents with adult Sunday School classes, teachers, and members.**
- **Connect teachers of siblings from the same family so the whole family is considered and has their needs addressed.**
- **Consider providing parent sessions** in the form of conferences, training opportunities, and chances for them to give feedback. Guidelines should include items such as the following:
  > Make the sessions relational.
  > Be positive.
  > Make each session worth the parents' time. Share plenty of information and clarify as needed.
  > Limit distractions. One way is to provide good programming for the children during the adult conference time.
  > Choose important and relevant topics.
  > Offer quality input from a knowledgeable facilitator, leader, or trainer.
- **Help parents see the value of regular church involvement.**
  > Consistency in church attendance aids in relationship building.
  > Church time serves as a special time for the family.
  > Partnering with teachers gives parents helpers in the faith walk.
  > Families can develop friendships with other like-minded families.
- **Provide and involve families in events such as picnics,** kids' talent-hobby night, music, and/or missions emphases, and so forth.

- **Operate out of pure motives.** Desire for each child and his or her parents to know and love Jesus better!

## What are some excellent strategies that can aid in building a strong family ministry?

- **A parent-child dedication meeting.** If parents wish to participate in a parent-child dedication service at the beginning of their child's life, request that they attend a brief, simple session. During the meeting explain what this event signifies, how the parents may follow up at home, the importance of regular church attendance, the involvement of the parents in the spiritual growth of their child, and ways your ministry is available to assist and nurture families.
- **Parenting sessions.** Regularly offer parent sessions which provide training, encouragement, and a time for questions and feedback.
- **A ministry newsletter.** Maintain consistent communication with parents through a ministry newsletter. Make the newsletter available by several methods such as the church's Web site, e-mail, blogs, regular mail, and bulletin boards.
- **A parent session for each parent whose child will be involved in a new believer class or experience.** This is an opportunity to help parents understand how they can explain the plan of salvation to their children and how they can help their children grow spiritually.
- **An open-door policy.** Inform parents of your availability to them and of your desire to help meet their family's needs. According to your schedule, communicate when you can best converse with them including office hours, hall visits, e-mail, or phone.
- **Parent input.** Invite and encourage parent input regarding your ministry. Consider developing a task group that includes parents, teachers of preschoolers and children, and other interested adults in the church. These adults can serve as your idea group, as encouragers, and as prayer supporters.

Because the job you do is so important for everyday life and for eternity, you must develop ways to become connected to the families of the kids to whom you minister. You owe it to the boys and girls. You owe it to the Lord to make every effort to serve families well. Jesus loved families so much that He chose to be a part of one when He dwelt among us!

*Jeanne Burns*

# Chapter 33
# How Do I Minister in Times of Crisis?

For I was hungry and you gave Me something to eat; I was thirsty and you gave Me something to drink; I was a stranger and you took Me in; I was naked and you clothed Me; I was sick and you took care of Me; I was in prison and you visited Me. Matthew 25:35-36

Celebrating with a family when a new child is born or a child has accepted Christ are probably the greatest joys you will experience in your ministry. But there will also be times you will be called on to minister to families in times of crisis. The mandate to minister in these difficult times is found in Matthew 25:40 when Christ said, "Whatever you did for one of the least of these brothers of Mine, you did for Me."

## What are times of crisis in kids' lives?
➤ terminal illness of the child or a family member
➤ birth of a sibling
➤ death of a child or family member
➤ separation or divorce of parents
➤ moving away or moving to a new home
➤ job loss of a parent
➤ natural disaster
➤ terrorist attack

## What do I need to know about ministering in times of crisis?
• **Acknowledge your awareness of the situation.** Communicate personally with the family. Make a phone call to express your concern. Arrange a visit to express face-to-face words of empathy and care. Assure the family of your continued prayers.
• **Determine in conversation with the parents the level of awareness the child has of the situation.** It is not your responsibility to get ahead of parents in informing children of reality. At the same time, you might need to encourage parents to share the truth with their child simply and forthrightly. Children are very perceptive. They can pick up on parents' moods and feelings quite well. They often overhear conversations or parts of conversations and their imagination may run rampant and give them more anguish and pain than the truth would.

- **Give opportunity for the child involved to talk about his or her understanding and feelings.** Express your concern to the child. Allow responses, but do not try to get the child to talk if he hesitates. A simple statements such as "This must be frightening to you," might help him to express his personal grasp of the gravity of the situation.
- **Do not underestimate a child's ability to cope with a crisis.** Children do not communicate their concerns and emotions in the same way as adults. There will be times of frequent laughter and play. Such behavior is the normal "language" children use to relieve themselves of their responses to painful, ongoing experiences.
- **Offer hope and promise.** Find ways to convey hope for the future. Younger children often feel alone or neglected when another family member is requiring the energies and time of parents and/or siblings. You have an opportunity to give friendship, love, care, and hope. Do so with the collaboration of parents by offering to spend time with the child. This could be a huge gift to the parents as well as the child.

## How do I minister in times of personal illness?

- Send a get-well card with a brief note expressing your concern.
- Call the home to let a child know that he was missed.
- Give an inexpensive gift to lift a child's spirit.
- Share words of comfort.
- Prepare meals for the family.
- Pray for the child in teaching sessions.

## How do I minister in times of family illness?

- Send get-well cards to the child's relative who is ill.
- Call regularly to check on the status of the one who is sick.
- Pray for the child's relative during your teaching session.
- Prepare meals/snacks and deliver with a hand-written note.
- Offer to run errands for the family if a parent is ill.

## How do I minister in times of death?

- Be available, but don't worry about talking a lot.
- Answer questions even if your answer is, "I don't understand either!"
- Avoid saying, "God took your grandmother to heaven because He loved her." This may be confusing to a child who is in the early stages of learning about God and about his relationship with God.
- Keep on hand a good children's book that deals appropriately with death to help comfort the child.
- Make a brief visit. Consider reading the book with the child.

## How do I minister during times of separation and divorce?

- Be available to assure a child that he is loved. Children often carry a burden of guilt when parents divorce or separate.
- Explain to a child that she did not cause her parents' problems.
- Offer a class for children on how to handle their parents' divorce.

## How do I minister when a child is moving?

- Talk about the excitement of new opportunities. Emphasize what will be gained and minimize what will be lost.
- Suggest ways to keep in touch with friends.
- Organize a way to say good-bye with a simple card or party.
- Mail a "thinking of you" card to the child's new address.

## How do I minister when children have issues at school?

- Children may never approach you about problems in school. However, remind children that you are available to talk.
- Eat lunch with children at school to let them know you care. Be sure to have the parents' and school's approval.
- Attend a child's sporting or other events.

## How do I minister when a parent loses a job?

- Be available to talk.
- Don't ask probing questions.
- Affirm that you will be praying for the family.
- Explore with the family how the church can help meet any physical or financial needs through the church's benevolence care.

## How do I minister in times of natural and man-made disasters?

- Find out what a family needs to meet their physical needs.
- Talk to children about what has happened.
- Listen to children as they express their fears.
- Reassure children that they are not alone.
- Give stuffed animals to young children for comfort.
- Give older children a journal to write down their feelings.

Your task as a leader who works with kids is to support families when a crisis happens. Even though you pray for children and their families to be safe, be prepared and willing to help as you depend on God's strength to guide you through times of crisis ministry.

*Cindy Lumpkin and Jerry Vogel*

# Acknowledgments

The LifeWay Kids Team wishes to thank the following people for their contributions to *Kids Ministry 101*.

- **Sheri Babb** *is a retired preschool ministry specialist for the Baptist General Convention of Oklahoma.*
- **Mary Ann Bradberry** *serves in the Mom to Mom ministry at Lakehills Church, Austin, Texas. Mary Ann is a freelance writer and conference leader.*
- **Todd Capps** *serves part-time as children's minister at Tulip Grove Baptist Church, Hermitage, Tennessee. Todd is editorial project leader for Worship KidStyle.*
- **Kathy Collins** *teaches 4s–kindergartners at First Baptist Church, Dickson, Tennessee. Kathy is a content editor for Bible Teaching for Kids Kindergarten resources.*
- **Danette Cravens** *most recently served as Preschool Ministry Coordinator for Rolling Hills Community Church, Franklin, Tennessee.*
- **Mary DePass** *teaches Kindergarten Sunday School at Greenforest Community Baptist Church, Decatur, Georgia.*
- **Erin Drawdy** *teaches 3-year-old Sunday School at Brentwood Baptist Church, Brentwood, Tennessee. Erin is the Internet Producer for LifeWay Kids and VBS.*
- **Ann Edwards** *teaches preschoolers at Brentwood Baptist Church, Brentwood, Tennessee. Ann is childhood ministry specialist for LifeWay Christian Resources.*
- **Bill Emeott** *teaches Sunday School and Children's Bible Drill at First Baptist Church, Nashville, Tennessee. Bill is lead childhood ministry specialist at LifeWay Christian Resources.*
- **David Garrard** *is minister to children at St. Matthews Baptist Church in Louisville, Kentucky. David also is an entertainer and magician.*
- **Carolle Green** *teaches children at First Baptist Church in Shreveport, Louisiana. Carolle retired from the Louisiana Baptist Convention where she was responsible for children's ministries.*
- **Landry R. Holmes** *teaches children at First Baptist Church, Goodlettsville, Tennessee. Landry is a managing director of Childhood Ministry Publishing, LifeWay Christian Resources.*
- **Jeff Land** *serves in multiple areas of children's ministry at Springfield Baptist Church in Springfield, Tennessee. Jeff is editorial project leader for LifeWay Preteens.*
- **Judy H. Latham** *is the assistant division director for Grades 4–6 at First Baptist Church, Nashville, Tennessee. Judy is a managing director of Childhood Ministry Publishing, LifeWay Christian Resources.*
- **Cindy Leach** *is minister to children at North Richland Hill Baptist Church, North Richland Hills, Texas.*
- **Cindy Lumpkin** *teaches 5th grade Sunday School at Forest Hills Baptist Church, Nashville, Tennessee. Cindy is the editorial project leader for childhood ministry and leadership resources at LifeWay Christian Resources.*

- **Carlton S. McDaniel, Jr.** *is special ministry specialist, Church Strategies, LifeWay Christian Resources.*
- **Jan Marler** *teaches children at The Peoples Church in Franklin, Tennessee. Jan is a childhood ministry specialist for LifeWay Christian Resources.*
- **Ken Marler** *has taught in TeamKid at the Peoples Church in Franklin, Tennessee. Ken is a Network Partnership specialist at LifeWay Christian Resources.*
- **Morlee Maynard**, *DEdMin, is the leader of the Mobilization Team at Forest Hills Baptist Church, Nashville, Tennessee.*
- **Gary Nicholson**, *AIA, is director of the church architecture department of LifeWay Christian Resources. Gary is a member at Rolling Hills Community Church, Franklin, Tennessee.*
- **Starr Nolan** *has taught preschoolers at First Baptist Church, Nashville, Tennessee. Starr is the content editor for the 3s–Pre-Kindergarten Bible Teaching for Kids resources.*
- **Shelley Pierce** *is director of children's ministry at Towering Oaks Baptist Church in Greenville, Tennessee.*
- **Tim Pollard** *teaches 6th grade boys in Sunday School at First Baptist Church Mount Juliet, Tennessee. Tim is editorial project leader for children's dated resources at LifeWay Christian Resources.*
- **Randy Smith** *teaches children's Sunday School, TeamKID, and leads in a summer day camp at Crystal Lake Baptist Church in Burnsville, Minnesota.*
- **Klista Storts** *is interim preschool minister First Baptist Church, Nashville, Tennessee. Klista is a childhood ministry specialist for LifeWay Christian Resources.*
- **Theresa Thomas** *teaches children in music and Bible Drill at First Baptist Church in Sebring, Florida.*
- **Helen Tindel** *teaches first grade Sunday School at Broadmoor Baptist Church in Shreveport, Louisiana. Helen has served on church staffs in Louisiana and Mississippi.*
- **Thomas Sanders** *is Childhood Ministry Director, Master of Arts in Christian Education Program and Assistant Professor of Christian Education and Childhood Ministry at Dallas Baptist University.*
- **Clara Mae VanBrink** *teaches 4-year-old Sunday School at First Baptist Church, Canton, Georgia. Clara Mae is a conference leader and motivational speaker.*
- **Jerry Vogel** *teaches kindergarten Sunday School at Brentwood Baptist Church, Brentwood, Tennessee. Jerry is the director of Childhood Ministry Publishing at LifeWay Christian Resources.*
- **R. Scott Wiley** *teaches 1st–3rd third grade choir and kindergartners in Sunday School at Tulip Grove Baptist Church, Hermitage, Tennessee. Scott is editorial project leader for preschool dated resources at LifeWay Christian Resources.*
- **Janet Hamm Williams** *is a retired childhood ministry specialist of the Arkansas Baptist State Convention.*
- **Jerry Wooley** *teaches VBS at Two Rivers Baptist Church, Nashville, Tennessee. Jerry is the Vacation Bible School ministry specialist for LifeWay Christian Resources.*

# Kids Ministry 101 CD-ROM Items

1. LifeSpan Spiritual Development
2. Levels of Biblical Learning™
3. Levels of Bible Skills
4. Kids Ministry Strategy
5. Kids Ministry Checklist
6. Leader Job Descriptions for Kids Ministry
7. Tips for Kids Ministry Leaders
8. 11 Steps to a Successful Kids Ministry
9. Kids Ministry in a Small Church
10a. Screening Form
10b. Release Form
11. 40 Easy Teacher Appreciation Ideas
12. Safety Guidelines
13. Preschool Room Safety Checklist
14–15. Cleaning Surfaces/Cleaning Materials
16–17. Washing Hands/Hygiene
18. Safe and Unsafe Plants
19. Kids Ministry Budget Worksheet
20. ABCs of Getting the Word Out
21. Basic Equipment List
22. Preschool Education Space
23. Children's Education Space
24. Basic Resources for Kids Ministry
25. Resource Rescue
26. Planning Leadership Meetings
27. 10 Quick Training Tips
28. 3 Kids Ministry Training Events
29. Evaluating Curriculum
30. Setting Up Bible-Teaching Experiences in a Non-Traditional Space
31. Meeting the Cultural Needs of Children
32. Characteristics of Preschoolers and Children
33. Do Babies Matter?
34. Ministry Organizational Chart
35. FIRST CONTACT
36. 16 Great Ways to Say Welcome
37. Planning Vacation Bible School
38. Ideas for Special Events for Children
39. Kids Retreats 101
40. Tips for Summer Planning
41. Day Camping in 9 Easy Steps